To my sons, Max and Jack.
Follow your dreams and they will lead you to great things.

ALADDIN
An imprint of Simon & Schuster
Children's Publishing Division
1230 Avenue of the Americas
New York, NY 10020

BEYOND WORDS
20827 N.W. Cornell Road, Suite 500
Hillsboro, Oregon 97124–9808
503-531-8700 / 503-531-8773 fax
www.beyondword.com

This Beyond Words/Aladdin edition August 2016

For information about special discounts for bulk purchases, please contact
Simon & Schuster Special Sales at 1-866-506-1949 or business@simonandschuster.com.

The Simon & Schuster Speakers Bureau can bring authors to your live event.
For more information or to book an event contact the Simon & Schuster Speakers
Bureau at 1-866-248-3049 or visit our website at www.simonspeakers.com.

Editor: Lindsay S. Easterbrooks-Brown
Annalisa Sparrow, Kristin Thiel
E. Blum
Design: William H. Brunson Typography Services
The text of this book was set in Adobe Bembo Standard.

Manufactured in the United States of America 0716 FFG

2 1

Library of Congress Cataloging-in-Publication Data

Patricia, author.
to be a leader? : an awesome guide to becoming a head honcho /

New York : Aladdin ; Hillsboro, Oregon : Beyond Words, 2016. |
want | Description based on print version record and CIP data
; resource not viewed.

6000046 (print) | LCCN 2015040667 (ebook) |
(eBook) | ISBN 9781582705484 (hardback) |
(paperback)
ip—Juvenile literature. | BISAC: JUVENILE NONFICTION
NONFICTION / Social Science / Politics & Government. |
ON / School & Education.
4 (print) | LCC BF637.L4 W66 20016 (ebook) |

lccn.loc.gov/2016000046

So, You Want to Be a Leader?

An Awesome Guide to Being a Head Honcho

Patricia W

ALADDIN
New York London Toro.

tr
Be
reg

For
Simo

The Si
For mo
Bureau

Managin
Editors: E
Design: Sar
Compositio
The text of t

Manufactured

10 9 8 7 6 5 4 3

Library of Cong
Names: Wooster,
Title: So, you want
Patricia Wooster.
Description: New Y
Series: Be what you
provided by publishe
Identifiers: LCCN 201
ISBN 9781481438445
ISBN 9781582705477
Subjects: LCSH: Leaders
/ Careers. | JUVENILE
JUVENILE NONFICTI
Classification: LCC BF637.
DDC 303.3/4—dc23
LC record available at http://

CONTENTS

1

Choosing to Be a Leader

Imagine standing in front of a group of people and inspiring them with your words. Or working with a team of people to achieve a common goal. Are you interested in politics or law enforcement? What about social causes or the environment? Coaching? Would you like your decisions to impact education and help children? Maybe you're more interested in working in the corporate world or dreaming up the next medical or technological breakthrough.

Being a leader isn't about bossing people around and telling them what to do. It's not about making threats or being a jerk. A great leader is someone who inspires others to act to achieve a goal or fix a problem. You don't have to be the president of the United States or in charge of a big company to be a leader. Leadership opportunities are everywhere. Check out what it takes to be a leader and see if you're inspired to become the next great success—even within your own family.

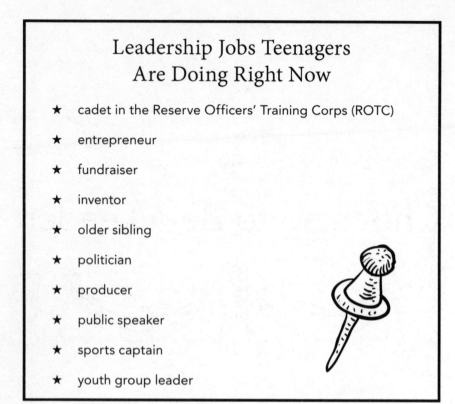

Leadership Jobs Teenagers Are Doing Right Now

★ cadet in the Reserve Officers' Training Corps (ROTC)

★ entrepreneur

★ fundraiser

★ inventor

★ older sibling

★ politician

★ producer

★ public speaker

★ sports captain

★ youth group leader

Characteristics of a Great Leader

You Have a Vision

Do you like to set goals and figure out ways to obtain them? Are you good at getting people motivated or excited? Would you like to work with people who share your vision of  success and work as a team to make it come true? A leader lights the first spark and continues to fuel the fire for the organization. Others can feed off it and continue to grow, develop, and perform. The vision is the goal or ideas a person has for an organization. A leader is the person who organizes the team to make those goals a reality.

Leading Leaders

We can look at leaders throughout history and see why they were so successful. Most strong leaders are good at building relationships and at taking advantage of new opportunities. They never stop learning and are curious about new things. Whether leading a country, running a corporation, or helping others in another way, they all share a passion for what they do. See how many of these great leaders you know, and do an internet search on any who may not be familiar to you.

Warren Buffett: investment guru and founder of Berkshire Hathaway

James Hansen: activist raising awareness of global warming

Martin Luther King Jr.: leader of the civil rights movement

Vince Lombardi: coach for the Green Bay Packers

Nelson Mandela: South African president who united his country

Condoleezza Rice: first African American woman to become secretary of state

Howard Schultz: CEO of Starbucks

Mother Teresa: Nobel Peace Prize–winning nun who advocated for the poor and sick

Sam Walton: founder of Walmart and Sam's Club

Oprah Winfrey: media mogul and one of the most influential women in the world

You Know What You Know... and Don't Know

Are you aware of your strengths and your weaknesses? Do you know what you're really good at and what you're really crummy at? Are you willing to ask for help when you need it and help others when they need your assistance? Do you look for new things  to learn and ways to beef up your skills? A great leader knows how to use a team's strengths. You're not afraid to admit you don't know everything. Using your teammates' skills makes the entire team stronger and makes people more invested in the vision. A leader should want every member to feel important.

You Are Confident

Do you know how to make decisions and stick to them? Once you make those decisions, do you feel good about them and not spend a lot of time second-guessing yourself? Can you trust your gut feelings? Great leaders are the decision makers and need to feel good about their decisions, so their teammates feel good about them too. Sometimes leaders will use a combination of information, experience, and natural intuition to guide their decision making.

You Have a Sense of Humor and a Positive Attitude

Are you upbeat? Can you bring people's spirits up when they are feeling down? Can you laugh at yourself and learn from your mistakes? A great leader knows things don't always go as planned. A positive attitude will keep your team motivated and productivity levels high. Nobody benefits from a negative environment, and everybody will be more committed to achieving success if they enjoy what they're doing.

> Before you are a leader, success is all about
> growing yourself. When you become a leader,
> success is all about growing others.[1]
> —JACK WELCH, FORMER CEO OF GENERAL ELECTRIC

You Are a Connector

Are you good at building relationships? Do you know whom to talk to when you need something? A great leader builds a network of people who can help support the team's vision. For example, if you're trying to raise money for your school, you want to network with local businesses, parents, and school clubs to help get the word out on your fundraising project. Networking skills keep you connected to your community, friends, and other people you meet along the way.

SPOTLIGHT

Dora Thewlis

What were you doing at age ten? Most likely you were spending your weekdays at elementary school and your weekends playing with friends and family. If you were Dora Thewlis you were at work, so you could help put food on the table. Thewlis was born in Yorkshire, England, in 1890 into a working class family that included her parents and six siblings. At age ten she began working as a weaver in a mill. At this time in history many industrial jobs were worked by women and children, and the working conditions were terrible. Impoverished children had to grow up fast in these days and received minimal schooling before their parents sent them off to a factory so they could earn a living to help their families with food and home expenses.

At the age of sixteen Thewlis was inspired by a speech she heard by Emmeline Pankhurst about women's suffrage, which is a woman's right to vote. She immediately joined the Women's Social and Political Union (WSPU) because they were the leading organization in the United Kingdom campaigning for women's suffrage. On March 8, 1907, the House of Commons rejected a bill allowing women who owned property the right to vote. Twelve days later hundreds of women stormed Parliament in protest. Seventy-five suffragettes were arrested including sixteen-year-old Thewlis.

The next day the front page of the paper showed a shouting Thewlis being arrested by two police officers. She was nicknamed the "Baby Suffragette" because of her young age. She kept the media captivated with her confidence and strong beliefs in the suffrage movement. In prison she was treated like a child and the government blamed her actions on poor parenting. This showed the great divide between the working class and the upper class where children didn't work, but were coddled. Thewlis became a leader within the movement of young working girls seeking the same rights and treatment as men. Their passion and hope for a better future gave them the confidence to lead women to organize and demand the right to vote.

Name: Ollie Forsyth
Age: 17
Job (when not studying!): Founder
of Ollie's Shop and *The Budding*
Entrepreneur

Ollie Forsyth was not willing to let dyslexia and being bullied get him down. In 2010, at the age of twelve, he began selling friendship bracelets to his family and friends. He later expanded this to an online shop to sell all types of affordable accessories. In November of 2014, he launched an online magazine called *The Budding Entrepreneur*, which provides tips, tricks, and inspiration to people who would like to create their own businesses. In addition to growing his business, Ollie enjoys restoring classic cars and supporting his favorite charities. Read on to find out why Ollie isn't willing to let any obstacle slow him down in building his empire.

Describe your businesses.
I started my first business in 2010, Ollie's Shop, an online gift shop for teenagers. I made the products fun and inexpensive. We sell belts, wallets, bracelets, and necklaces. Our price range is five to thirty-five pounds. I started OllieShop.co.uk. My second business I have started recently is *The Budding Entrepreneur* magazine, an online subscription magazine for entrepreneurs. It gives you all the tools you need as a start-up. It is fifteen pounds a year. This is affordable to most people, and by paying that, you can have your business up and going for fifteen pounds! On the site, we have all the essentials for starting a business, advice, business tools, entrepreneurial stories, and lots of celebrities! You can see the site at TBEmagazine.com.

I have been in over forty newspapers and magazines, and none of those magazines gave you the steps toward starting your business. All the newspapers covered heavy content. I created something that gives you more advice, but simpler. I covered all my start-up costs before even starting! Advertising is very big!

How did you get started?

I started with nothing. I am very dyslexic and was badly bullied and cyberbullied at a school in Dorset, United Kingdom Milton  Abbey School. I attend Bruern Abbey School, a special-needs school in Oxfordshire. I wouldn't be here today without it. They helped me with my dyslexia a lot. Being bullied and cyberbullied at school has really had an effect on my life. It's driven me to who I am today, but I never clocked in why [that] bunch of boys did it to me. I have no contact with those boys anymore. If people don't have time for me, I don't have time for them. Why should I?

What challenges have you faced by leading a company as a teen?

I have faced many challenges. My social life has been limited because I am so determined to make it to the top. My ethos has always been to work as hard as you can, and make as much money as you can, as fast as you can, for as long as you can. I say these words to myself every day since watching Peter Jones with Richard Dawson. Those are his exact words.

I think having a business as a teen is great. You learn so much and network with some amazing people. I am net-working with multimillionaires to successful entrepreneurs to start-ups. I will get my foot in the door to every single person who I think can help me with my business, and who I think I can help.

What leadership qualities do you find are the most important when running a business?

When leading a business, you are constantly in the public eye. People always want to know what you are doing. You want to lead your team with respect and to also be generous. Always give something back. I commute to my college every day. I see three to four homeless people every day. If I walk past them, I will empty my pockets and give them all my change. Why? This is not for publicity at all. It's because nobody else is giving these unsheltered people support, so if no one else is, somebody has to keep these people fit, well, and healthy.

What leaders do you look up to?
I look up to many entrepreneurs, like Richard Branson, Lord Sugar, and Donald Trump. When starting a business, always have someone you aspire to be. It will make you so much more motivated. It will make you driven, and you will have the adrenaline inside you to succeed in life.

What advice would you give teens who are interested in starting their own businesses?
I could write a whole book on advice, but the best advice I can give is to get out there as fast as you can. If school is not your forte, get out of there, and go enjoy what you want to do.★ Don't be afraid of failure. You will fail at some point in your life, but it's good to fail because you learn from it and you can pass the advice on to fellow entrepreneurs. My final piece of advice would be don't let people undermine you. I was told I would never succeed in life by those bullies. Well, I am now earning in the five figures, and they are not earning a single penny. Anything is possible. You just have to put your mind to it!

✪ ✪

★ The views expressed here are those of the interviewee and not necessarily shared or endorsed by the author or publisher.

Do You Have What It Takes to Lead?

How are your leadership skills? Have people told you that you're a natural-born leader? Or are you looking to develop the skills you need for a leadership position? Being a leader is a big responsibility. A lot of people will look to you for direction and advice, so you need to prepare yourself. The first step is to take an honest assessment of your strengths and areas for improvement. This quiz will give you feedback on where you stand right now. For each statement, give yourself one of the following scores on a separate piece of paper:

1 = Never
2 = Rarely
3 = Sometimes
4 = Often true
5 = Always true

★   I always give 100 percent, even when no one is watching.

★   My friends trust me.

★   I always do what I say I'm going to do.

★   People look up to me.

★   I set goals and work to achieve them.

★   I share my beliefs with others.

★   I stick with things even when they get tough.

★   I plan for my future.

★ When I disagree with friends, I don't let it turn into a fight.

★ I speak up when something bothers me.

★ I can take constructive criticism.

★ My friends can be honest with me.

★ My friends respect me.

★ My friends don't talk about me behind my back.

★ I like to learn new things.

★ I have the skills to lead people.

★ I can make tough decisions.

★ I am willing to take risks.

★ I like to be the first to do something new.

★ If I believe in something, I won't take no for an answer.

Add up your score and see what you can do to become a stronger leader!

1–60 Points: You are interested in becoming a leader and are ready to learn new skills. Think of steps you can take to learn something new every day. Find activities that increase your self-confidence, strengthen your communication skills, and excite you. Learn everything you can about leaders you admire and copy their behavior. Sign up for the debate team, student government, or clubs that let you practice leadership skills.

61–80 Points: You've got leadership skills and know how to use them. Now it's time to fine-tune those skills. Look for new challenges where you can lead others. This may be at school, a part-time job, youth group, or a volunteer center. Along the way, ask for feedback from everyone! This will help you to make changes and improvements, so you can become a better leader.

81–100 Points: You are a leader! People look up to you for guidance and direction. You are confident and not afraid to make difficult decisions. Make sure to encourage those around you to be a part of decision making and offer input. That's part of building a great team.

✪✪✪✪✪✪✪✪✪✪✪✪✪✪✪✪

Name: Emily Raleigh
Age: 20
Job (when not studying!): Founder of Smart Girls Group

Emily Raleigh had no idea when she sat down to write a high school survival guide for her younger sister that it would lead to a company with a magazine, website, conferences, and online classes. As a sophomore at Fordham University (class of 2016) in New York, she divides her time between her studies and the Smart Girls Group. In 2013, she won a Kenneth Cole Foundation AWEARNESS Grant, which is given to student-led social organizations. Currently, the Smart Girls Group consists of over two hundred girls from ten different countries ranging from high school age to twenty-five years old.

Describe the Smart Girls Group.
Smart Girls Group is a multiplatform community that provides products, resources, and opportunities that empower women and girls. We arm ambitious females with the tools that they need to succeed in all facets of life on their own terms, all in

a unique sisterhood environment. We have a monthly digital magazine called *Smart Girls Guide*; a daily online magazine; campus chapters throughout the US, Canada, and Europe; online classes; an online community; online shop; book club; live events; and various leadership programs. Our goal is to provide girls with [a] Smart Girl option for everything they do throughout their day, whether that is what they read, who they hang out with, or how they spend their free time. The top priority is definitely the sisterhood aspect, which is connecting girls across the globe, and that's definitely my favorite part about it. We have over one thousand Smart Girl Sisters working on Smart Girls Group, and they are from fifty states and forty-four countries.

How did it get started?
The Smart Girls Group idea really started when I was a little girl. I would walk downstairs every morning after putting on my outfit for school and ask, "Mommy, do I look smart?" I was raised on the concept of the Smart Girl. With that in mind, I wrote a book for my freshman sister, Sophie, during my senior year of high school that was a how-to guide for surviving and succeeding in high school. I gave it to her for Christmas, and my family really wanted me to get it published. I wanted to do something that would be more than just a book, something that was continuous. So on New Year's Day, I made my New Year's resolution to start the Smart Girls Group.

We initially had nine girls involved and released a small magazine that we planned to only be ten pages long. Soon enough, the sisterhood began to grow, and so did our products. What keeps us moving are the girls, and we truly have a group of girls who will change the world.

How do you manage college and running your own company at the same time?

It definitely isn't easy! I truly could not do what I do without my Smart Girls Group teammates. Our staff is an incredibly driven, passionate group of women who I feel very fortunate to get to work with. I have learned how to delegate and prioritize. My planner is practically an extension of myself, and I take scheduling very seriously. I'm convinced you can balance everything if you can schedule it. The key is sticking to that schedule, which can be the hardest part.

What do you think makes a strong leader?

A strong leader is someone who knows how to invest well. No, I'm not talking about financial investments (although that can be important for some leaders). I'm talking about life investments. Every second of every day is an opportunity to move forward. A strong leader knows how to invest his/her time in endeavors that will have the highest return on investment, whether that is empowering a team in hard times or answering emails within twenty-four hours to ensure customers feel important. Time is the most valuable asset for every leader, and the strongest leaders are those who best invest their time.

What skills can students start developing now to become a leader in the future?

Be a leader in every aspect of life! Don't let others dictate what choices you make. Take on leadership roles in an organization, club, or activity that excites you. Pursue your passions, whatever they may be. Set yourself apart from the rest in all that you do.

What current or past leaders have inspired you and why?

So many! I have always admired my nana and pop, who are both entrepreneurs. Their dedication and drive, partnered with their ability to see life beyond work, have always inspired me. I hope some day I have my dad's marketing skills. I'm constantly calling him, asking for advice on how we can get a new supporter or a new client, and I truly haven't met someone who can sell something the way he can. My mom is a teacher, and her patience astounds me, and I try to channel her when I get frustrated.

Outside my family, I am incredibly inspired by Richard Branson. Is there an entrepreneur who doesn't consider him a role model? I loved reading his books, especially when I first started expanding Smart Girls Group during my freshman year of college, because his books and blog gave me a sense of confidence in my vision of Smart Girls, even if only few could see it at the time.

I am deeply inspired by Lauren Bush Lauren. Her efforts with FEED are nothing shy of incredible. She was the first entrepreneur I looked to when I started Smart Girls Group, and when we started planning Smart Girls Summit, she was the first person I invited to come as a speaker. There is nothing more motivating for me than seeing another woman entrepreneur not just creating a wildly successful business but also creating major social change in the process.

What advice would you give students who are looking to gain leadership experience right now?

Ask a lot of questions. I have found that experienced leaders love to support aspiring leaders. Educate yourself on the paths they took to become leaders. If you admire a leader who is difficult to contact, read their interviews and books. There is so much to learn, and the more you educate yourself, the better leader you will be.

✪✪✪✪✪✪✪✪✪✪✪✪✪✪✪✪✪✪✪✪✪✪✪

The Types of Governments around the Globe

★ **authoritarian:** absolute obedience to authority, ruled by a president
examples: Armenia, Vietnam, and Egypt

★ **commonwealth:** all people have a say in the government, ruled by a prime minister
examples: Australia, the Bahamas, and Dominica

★ **communist:** a ruling party guided by Marxist-Leninism hoping to achieve socialism, ruled by a president
examples: Cuba, China, and Laos

★ **constitutional:** follows the policies stated in their constitution, ruled by a president or prime minister
examples: Iceland, United States, and Germany

★ **ecclesiastical:** based on the theology of the Christian church, ruled by a monarchy
example: Vatican City-State

★ **Islamic republic:** governed by Islamic law, ruled by a president
examples: Iran, Pakistan, and the Gambia

★ **monarchy:** governed by one or more people who rule for life like kings and queens
examples: United Kingdom, Belgium, and Nation of Brunei

★ **parliamentary government:** based on an executive and legislative branch and governed by a head of state and head of government
examples: Africa, Asia, and the Pacific

2

Get Political

So, now that you've decided to explore leadership opportunities, where do you begin? With a look at the many different places that need a great leader! This book will provide you with information on the most common career fields that need leaders. Some of these fields focus on government and law enforcement, while others involve education and humanitarian efforts. Whatever interests you may have, you will find a need for great leadership skills.

What is the one quality that all leaders have? They all share a vision of something that needs to be fixed or needs improvement, and they act upon that vision. Many people think of government when they think about jobs requiring leadership. The most visible job is president of the United States, but it's not the only important political job. The government is made up of millions of people with leadership roles as diplomats, representatives, senators, and Supreme Court justices. Not to mention roles in various government departments like the Internal Revenue Service, the Department of Transportation, and the United States Postal Service. Each of the various branches, departments, and agencies requires people with leadership skills to deliver and communicate the overall goals and vision for the group.

Types of Government Leaders

The foundation of the government is built upon three distinct, but equally powerful, branches: the legislative, the executive, and the judicial. There's no doubt that you've studied the United States Constitution and why a system of checks and balances keeps the power divided among many people. What you may not have studied is how these elected officials go about getting their jobs. Read up on the following governmental branches and see if any of them inspire you to start making your own campaign banners!

Legislative Branch

This is the lawmaking branch, made up of the House of Representatives and the Senate. The House of Representatives has 435 members who represent the people who live within their congressional districts. The members only serve two-year terms, so re-election is always right around the corner. In the Senate, each state has two representatives, regardless of the state's size. Senators are lucky because they come up for re-election only every six years.

If making laws sounds exciting to you then go ahead and get started at your school. Start a campaign and run for student council. As a student government candidate you'll go through a similar process when trying to get elected. You'll want to get your name on the ballot, so you need to start telling your classmates what you'll do for them once you get into office. Ask around and find out what type of changes students would like to see at your school. After you get your name on the ballot, you are headed for the general election. By this time, you're pretty familiar with giving speeches, and hopefully voters have a good idea of what you believe in. Once you're elected, it's important to make all your campaign promises come true. Don't forget . . . you represent the people!

> **A leader takes people where they want to go.**
> **A great leader takes people where they don't**
> **necessarily want to go, but ought to be.**[1]
> —ROSALYNN CARTER

Executive Branch

The executive branch has the important responsibility of carrying out the laws established by the legislative branch. Many people think of the president when they think of this branch, but this branch holds many leadership roles. It consists of the president, the vice president, and fifteen cabinet members nominated by the president to run the executive departments. These departments consist of:

Department of Agriculture: regulates food safety and the farming industry

Department of Commerce: regulates everything having to do with money

Department of Defense: includes all armed forces

Department of Education: ensures everyone has access to an education

Department of Energy: monitors and improves energy sources

Department of Health and Human Services: focuses on Americans' health

Department of Homeland Security: fights the war on terror

Department of Housing and Urban Development: provides affordable housing

Department of the Interior: protects natural resources

Department of Justice: enforces laws

Department of Labor: protects workers' safety and rights

Department of State: advises the president on foreign policy

Department of Transportation: establishes roads and transportation safety

Department of the Treasury: keeps the nation's finances in check

Department of Veterans Affairs: provides medical care and benefits to injured military personnel

SPOTLIGHT

John F. Kennedy

If you ask your parents, "Which US president was the most charismatic?" more often than not they will say, "John F. Kennedy." Born in Brookline, Massachusetts, in 1917, Kennedy was raised by a prominent family with long political ties. He became interested in social and political issues while attending Harvard University. Upon graduation, he enlisted in the US Navy and earned the Purple Heart and the Navy and Marine Corps Medal for his rescue efforts after his boat was hit by a Japanese destroyer.

By 1946, Kennedy felt the pull of politics and was elected to the US House of Representatives by the Democratic Party. He found it to be a little boring and wished to make a larger contribution, so he set out for the Senate in 1952. After many years of sitting on committees and working on civil rights bills, he decided to run for president, and won the election.

His 1961 inaugural speech is still taught in classrooms and is as famous now as it was back then. His inspirational message started with, "Ask not what your country can do for you; ask what you can do for your country." This became the theme of his presidency as he made one contribution after another to United States history. His legacy includes establishing the Peace Corps, which is a volunteer organization to help other countries. He averted the Cuban Missile Crisis, which could've led to a nuclear war. And he passed the 1964 Civil Rights Act, which gave educational, voting, and facility rights and access to all citizens. He was assassinated during a political trip that same year.

Kennedy was able to unite many different types of people based on his communication skills, sincerity, and interest in social justice. Many books and articles have been devoted to his popularity and his presidency. If you are interested in a career in politics or social services, you should read up on this president. Who knows— maybe some of his idealism will rub off on you!

Judicial Branch

The judicial branch has the important job of interpreting the laws and deciding what they mean. It contains the highest court in the nation, called the United States Supreme Court. It contains a chief justice and eight associate judges who are all appointed by the president. They are appointed for life! They review cases appealed from the lower courts and make sure the laws were applied correctly. Every year they receive over 7,500 requests for cases to be reviewed. They pick only about 150 cases to examine.[2]

If this job sounds interesting, then you can go ahead and get started on your climb to the Supreme Court. Find a political cause through your school, like the student council, the debate team, or a fundraising group. If you want to look outside of your school, then you can volunteer at a campaign office and help out a local politician running for office. When it's time to go to college, a degree in political science or criminal justice, along with good grades, should set you on the path for law school.

After law school, you can join the district attorney's office or become a law clerk. Either way, it will be important to keep up with all of the new laws. Many people choose to become law professors or publish articles about the law. If you decide that being a judge is your calling, then you have options at the local, state, and national levels. These are either elected or appointed positions. Judges have the ultimate authority in the courtroom and have to be prepared to make tough legal decisions.

✪✪✪✪✪✪✪✪✪✪✪✪✪✪✪✪✪

Name: Jack Swan
Age: 19
Job (when not studying!): Deputy member of the United Kingdom Youth Parliament

A lot of people consider government the ultimate in leadership because often officials are chosen by their peers and make decisions that affect laws and policies. At nineteen years of age, Jack Swan, representing Essex County in England, is already at that high point. The Youth Parliament (YP) allows students ages eleven to eighteen to have an impact on social changes in the United Kingdom. There are over six hundred elected youth representatives and 230 deputy members. The idea is for youth to have a voice with their local and national government. Over a million youths have exercised their right to vote and have participated in the YP elections in the last two years. At the last House of Commons debate, the top issues discussed were voting rights starting at the age of sixteen, youth unemployment, and improved mental health services. By allowing the practice of democracy at such a young age, the United Kingdom is building its next generation of leaders.

Tell me about the United Kingdom Youth Parliament.
The United Kingdom Youth Parliament (UKYP) is an organization which campaigns on issues affecting young people. A lot of people misconstrue it as some kind of model Parliament, with youth versions of political parties sitting around and debating. It's not (thankfully); it's best described as a pressure group, with a very strong focus on engaging young people in deciding its campaigns. As a collective organization, it campaigns on large issues such as lowering the voting age to sixteen, but it also provides a support system and network for individual young people to campaign on issues in their communities—one particularly frequent issue is travel fares for young people.

What is your position with the YP, and how did you get your position?
I'm currently a deputy member of the Youth Parliament, and was a full member last year. In Essex, members of our county-wide organization—the Young Essex Assembly—may run for election to the UKYP subgroup and then are part of it for a two-year term. You spend one year as a full member, which entitles you to visit the summer annual sitting and the House

of Commons sitting in November, and another as a deputy member, which is more of a support role and (as the name suggests) a deputy, where you can fill in for a full member if they are unavailable.

What leadership skills have you gained from your involvement?

In the last few months, I became aware of members of the youth parliament who were dissatisfied with some of the scheduling choices of the organization, along with various other concerns and gripes about how things are run. I took it upon myself to create a debate within our Facebook page and through that recruited an informal group of MYPs [member YPs] interested in reforming certain elements of the organization. Coordinating twelve young people across the whole of Britain using purely the power of the internet was definitely a challenge! But it was a worthwhile one—despite the stress, being able to delegate roles, construct surveys with the other reformists and share them with the wider membership of UKYP, and draw up a fully researched proposal was an incredibly rewarding experience. Given the fact that online organization will be a huge part of our future lives, because of the rise of the internet and (as a young person) the difficulty in organizing and funding face-to-face meetings of large numbers of geographically disparate people, the reform exercise was a fantastic opportunity to build my skills in online team leadership.

What policies are you interested in?

When I first joined the Youth Parliament I was particularly keen on Votes at 16—which you'll discover is the hot topic of the Youth Parliament, once you chat with MYPs or see how energized by the topic they get at the House of Commons sitting. However, following the budget cuts to my local youth service in Essex (where 60 percent of our budget was removed), I've become far more engaged with the existential threat facing youth services across the country.

Youth services offer something for every young person: drug and alcohol support, sexual health information, music schools, career guidance, relationship advice, provision for youth careers, after-school and extracurricular activities, the organization and running of schemes like the National Citizen Service and Duke of Edinburgh—the list goes on and on. But most local authorities facing budget cuts see a lot of savings to be made by reducing or even scrapping youth services altogether (as has happened in Staffordshire). I'm extremely keen on seeing the introduction of statutory youth services, with clear government guidelines on their provision—rather than the current advice, which says they must merely be "sufficient . . . so far as is reasonably practicable."

Of course, what I should say is that, as a representative of young people in Essex, I am most keen on fighting for a living wage—which is what the results of 2014's Make Your Mark ballot says is the most popular policy locally!

What advice would you give teens who are interested in a career in politics?

It's never too early to get involved, so consider joining your local party and its national youth wing. But when it comes to youth voice—such as youth councils, forums, assemblies, or the wider UK Youth Parliament—be prepared to put your views to the side. You're joining these organizations to help young people, not yourself, so don't just sit around bashing your least favorite political party; start talking about what the issues facing young people locally are, and more importantly, what you can do to solve them. Politics is so much more than the color of the rosette you wear; politics is getting out on the street and working with people from every corner of the community to change things for the better. If you want to get involved in politics, engage yourself in the issues, not the parties, and throw yourself into meeting with councillors, with local people, with anyone—and make the change. You'll discover what politics really is, and I guarantee you'll be hooked.

How do you plan to apply the skills you've learned from YP in your future career?
Essex's youth services are moving to a commissioning-based model, so I'm planning to set up an organization to provide and support youth councils across the county. Organizing this will depend on the online leadership skills I mentioned earlier, but I'll also be sure to spread the commitment to (and methods of) consulting young people to best represent them, as well as finding the best avenues to get in touch with local councillors and other decision makers who can actually implement change.

✪✪✪✪✪✪✪✪✪✪✪✪✪✪✪✪✪✪✪✪✪✪✪✪

Get Educated and Get to Work!

The path to becoming a politician is different for every person. Many people who work in the government have college degrees in business, economics, or political science. After obtaining their four-year bachelor's degree, some go on to law school or to earn a master's degree in business. Nearly all politicians were involved with political parties and extracurricular activities during their college careers. Check out the following activities and internship opportunities to see how you can become involved right now.

Democratic National Committee (DNC)

If you plan on becoming a politician, then consider working for a political party now. This is as up close and personal as it gets for learning about political issues, campaigning, and raising the awareness for grassroots projects. As an intern you will get to assist in community outreach, tour Washington, DC offices, and attend weekly lunches with members of the DNC. For more information, go to democrats.org/groups/internships.

Republican National Committee (RNC)

Consider heading to Washington, DC, to take advantage of the many opportunities available to work for this political party. They have internship programs in the chairman's office, the press office, research, social media, strategy, and member services. Whatever interests you may have, this political party has a learning program for you. Descriptions can be found at gop.com/internships.

The Principality of Sealand: The World's Smallest Nation

Approximately seven miles off the shores of Britain sits the world's smallest country on international waters. Sealand is located on an abandoned sea fort built by Britain during World War II. It was founded in 1966 by Roy Bates, who moved his wife, two children, and some friends to the sea tower. In 1967, he romantically declared it a principality, so his wife could officially become a princess. You can read about a pirate invasion of Sealand, life on the water, and how you can become a count or countess of Sealand at sealandgov.org.

White House Internship Program

If you're looking for the ultimate political internship, then look no further than the White House! This leadership program is aimed at introducing youth to the executive office. Get exposed to many different public service jobs. On any given day as an intern you may write memos, attend staff meetings, and participate in service projects. Go to whitehouse.gov/about/internships to learn how to apply.

YMCA Youth & Government

Would you like an opportunity to learn about the issues affecting your own state? If so, you may enjoy getting together with other people your age to learn about upcoming bills that impact your community. You can attend state conferences and propose changes. Contact your local YMCA for more information. To get involved, visit ymca.net/be-involved.

SPOTLIGHT

Emma Watson

Whether you're a movie buff or not, you've probably heard of this British actress, model, designer, and humanitarian. Emma was born in 1990 and is best known for her role as Hermione Granger in the Harry Potter movie franchise from 2001 to 2011. The movies follow Hermione and her best friends Ron Weasley and Harry Potter on their adventures at the Hogwarts School of Witchcraft and Wizardry while they battle the evil Lord Voldemort. Now she is fighting a real-life battle to end gender inequality as a United Nations global goodwill ambassador.

How did a young girl go from being an actress to an ambassador who gives important speeches about global issues all over the world? She did it by having a passion for humanitarian work. At the beginning of her career she asked her fans to donate to UNICEF and volunteer at children's charities. She's served as an ambassador for the Campaign for Female Education (Camfed) and visited Zambia and Bangladesh to promote education for young girls. By lending her name and her time to countless charities over the years she became known for her humanitarian work.

After graduating from Brown University in 2014 with a degree in English Literature she decided to take on the role of a lifetime as a UN goodwill ambassador. She helped them launch the HeForShe campaign that asks men to take a stand against discrimination faced by women. By asking boys to join in the fight to end gender inequality she has redefined what it means to be a feminist. She wants to end the common association of feminism with "man-hating."[3] Instead she is presenting women's rights issues to men as an opportunity for them to secure equality for their moms, daughters, sisters, and friends. Her leadership is bringing national attention to this issue and bringing a new generation into the fight against gender inequality. Her role as the super-smart and tough Hermione in the Harry Potter series may have prepared her for her greatest role yet!

Student Government

For firsthand experience in leadership and democracy, you should consider participating in your school's student government. Student council's purpose is to work as a go-between for your classmates and the school administrators. In addition to discussing school rules and policies, you will plan fun events. Student government is usually in charge of spirit week, pep rallies, prom, and community outreach programs. Just like the United States government, your school government has many different types of jobs, and you should choose which to sign up for or campaign to do based on your interests. You can practice your leadership skills while making your school a better place to be by taking on one of these positions.

Student Body President

Do you have specific ideas for how to make your school a better place? Have you already held office in your student government or another school or community club? Then consider running for the highest student government position: president! During your campaign you will outline your goals for the upcoming year, and after you take office, your job will be to make those goals come true. As a representative of your classmates, you will be expected to keep the administrators informed as to the students' wants and needs.

Class Presidents

Would you like to represent your grade on issues concerning them? Every grade has its own president. In this position you will attend all of the student body president's meetings, plan social events for your grade, and resolve problems for your classmates.

Secretary

Do you have great communication skills? Are you a good listener and well organized? If so, serving as the secretary for your student government may be the perfect role for you. The secretary has the very important job of taking notes at all the student government meetings. The notes are a very important record of everything discussed and who is going to be in charge of various projects. Typically, the secretary will send a report of the meeting to all of the officers, so they can keep track of everything discussed.

Treasurer

Are you good with money? Do you know how to plan a budget and keep your spending in check? If so, you may enjoy being in charge of the student council's money as the treasurer. This is money raised through fundraising or school events that pays for school dances, programs, and other school expenses. The treasurer keeps records of all money that is received and spent and budgets for upcoming expenses. This is a very important job because many school groups count on these funds to pay for their events.

Historian

Do you like to clip newspaper articles, write about events, and organize scrapbooks? If so, you may want to serve as your student council's historian. Your job will be to document and photograph the year's events and projects. You will keep mementos, maintain records on the success of school parties and projects, and put together a scrapbook. The job may have you working with the school newspaper and yearbook staff. By the end of the year, you'll be a pro at organizing information and coordinating with different departments.

Name: Daniel Burgess
Job: Mayor of Zephyrhills, Florida,
and representative for State House
District 38

All it takes is one event to change your life, and for Danny Burgess, that event was the tragic terrorist attacks on September 11, 2001, at the World Trade Centers, the Pentagon, and in Pennsylvania. Those events motivated him to become a captain of the US Army and begin a life in politics. In 2005, he became the youngest elected politician in the state of Florida as a member of the Zephyrhills City Council. In 2013, at the age of twenty-seven, he became the city's youngest mayor. Now he's set his sights on representing his community in Tallahassee in his role in State House District 38. Check out his views on leadership and how you can start participating in politics right now!

How did you become interested in politics?
The tragic events of 9/11 put the rest of my life in focus for me. It was on that day, in a tenth-grade high school English classroom at Zephyrhills High School, that I realized that I wanted to lead a life of public service and try to make a difference in this world. That is why I decided to serve in our

armed forces, and that is why I ran for office at the age of eighteen.

What activities in high school prepared you for your career?
I was actively involved in student government and a member of the Zephyrhills Youth City Council.

Where do you see leadership opportunities for teens in your community?

As the mayor of the city of Zephyrhills, I helped to bring back the youth council, what was renamed the Mayor's Youth Council.

What challenges have you faced working in politics?

At the age of eighteen, I was elected to the Zephyrhills City Council as the youngest elected official in the state of Florida, as a freshman in college. There were a lot of questions about my "youth and inexperience."

You are never expected to know everything, nor should one pretend to. Don't be afraid to ask the important questions and seek guidance from those who do know about a certain topic of which you may be unfamiliar. God gave us two ears and one mouth for a reason; we should listen more than we speak, and we should never be afraid to learn.

Also, some of the greatest lessons and growth experiences in life are learned from the mistakes we make along the way. Use these lessons to become a stronger leader and do not be afraid to admit when you are wrong. People admire honesty and humility—it takes courage and shows your true character.

What personality traits make a great leader?

Courage, integrity, trustworthiness, humility, honesty, and honorability.

What advice would you give teens who are interested in politics?

I would tell them that they are not just the future—they are today. They have a voice and something to offer. Don't be afraid to let your voice be heard and be an active participant in your community. You only have one life to live, and you should set your sights on your goals and dreams and never look back. Be the positive change you want to see in this world.

✪✪✪✪✪✪✪✪✪✪✪✪✪✪✪✪✪✪✪✪✪✪✪✪

3

Protect Your Community

Do you like the idea of having the words *bravery* and *courage* as part of your job description? Would it make you happy to keep your community safe? That's great! Because law enforcement leaders have to make tough decisions during difficult situations. They are responsible for protecting citizens against criminals and in dangerous situations.

This job may sound exciting, but it's a serious job too. As a law enforcement leader, you'll need to keep your team's spirits and morale up. Their morale is how they feel about what they do. With life-and-death decisions on the line, it's important that officers believe in their mission. This is a job where trust is key. Your coworkers serve as your partners and backup during tense situations. Teamwork plays a major role in many situations where dispatchers, officers, the fire department, and paramedics work together to resolve a problem. A strong leader will lead by example, which sends a positive message to coworkers and the community.

Does all of this sound interesting? If so, it's time to learn about the many different law enforcement agencies that keep us safe. Whether you're interested in keeping your neighborhood safe, solving major crimes, serving your country, or protecting the environment, there's a job for you. Read on to see where you can put your leadership skills to work.

★✪✪✪✪✪✪✪✪✪✪✪✪✪✪✪

Name: William Johnson
Job: Executive director of the
National Association of Police
Organizations

The National Association of Police Organizations (NAPO) gives a unified voice to the law enforcement community by making sure members are represented when important decisions are made about their towns, communities, and states. In addition to helping to make and enforce laws, its members have established relief funds, awards programs, and safety programs for officers in the field. You can thank NAPO's members for the National Amber Alert Act, Fair Sentencing Act, and Family and Medical Leave Act, in addition to many other legislative programs. The executive director, William Johnson, offers great advice to those who are considering an exciting career in law enforcement.

Describe the National Association of Police Organizations.
NAPO is a coalition of police unions and associations from across the United States that serves to advance the interests of America's law enforcement community through

legislative and legal advocacy, political action, and education. Founded in 1978, NAPO now represents more than 1,000 police units and associations, 241,000 sworn law enforcement officers, and more than 100,000 citizens who share a common dedication to fair and effective crime control and law enforcement.

Why should someone interested in being a leader consider a career in law enforcement?

In my opinion, the fundamental components of good leadership are the same components that make good and successful police officers. These include a fundamental attitude of service and sacrifice in assisting others—a willingness to endure difficult and challenging circumstances in order to accomplish a greater good. Also, law enforcement personnel are generally regarded by the public as leaders in the community, and this engenders an ethos of living up to those expectations among many officers.

What leadership qualities are important for law enforcement officers to have?

A spirit of sacrifice, of service, of willingness to do the right thing even when it's tough. The ability to rise to challenges instead of giving up. The ability to keep plugging ahead even when discouraged by court decisions or failures by prosecutors to charge defendants after you've taken the time to solve the case and make the arrest. The ability to lead by example and persuasive communication, not forcing others to do what you want in every case, although it's important to note that force does sometimes need to be used. This brings up the importance of personal integrity, because officers are entrusted with great power and authority and work 24/7, often on their own.

What leadership opportunities or needs do you see in the future for law enforcement?

As long as there are human beings, there will be a need for some of us to stand up for and defend others who are not able to protect themselves. This is the unchanging core of the societal need for law enforcement and law enforcement officers. Although budgets, political leadership, methods of communications can and will all change over time, the need to serve others by enforcing the legitimately enacted laws of our communities will remain.

What type of experience does someone need to work with an organization like NAPO?

Our own membership is very broad and consists of officers, associations, citizens who want to support their police, surviving family members of officers who have died, police chaplains, and so on. Some have been involved in law enforcement for thirty or more years; some are brand new or even going through police academy now. So one doesn't need any particular type or scope of experience to join.

What advice would you give teens who are interested in a career in law enforcement?

Every police department in the United States has its own requirements for becoming an officer, but in general, I can tell you what most departments require.

To become a police officer or deputy sheriff, you usually have to be at least eighteen years old, and sometimes twenty-one years old. You will need a high school diploma, and many police departments now require two or four years of college. A driver's license with a good driving record is also usually required. Also, the officer cannot have been in serious trouble with the law before he or she applies for the position. Persons who are hired as police officers or deputies are sent to a special school called an academy, where they learn all the things a police officer needs to know. This includes the criminal law, safe driving, first aid, self-defense, and how to deal with many different types of people.

After several years of good work as a police officer, you can apply for a transfer or promotion to the rank of detective. Detectives are police officers or deputy sheriffs who specialize in collecting evidence, talking to witnesses, interviewing suspects, and solving crimes. Detectives also need to work closely with prosecutors to present their evidence in court to a judge and jury. Detectives may also go to special schools to learn how to solve different types of crimes. Our organization, the National Association of Police Organizations, represents police officers and detectives from all over the country, and I think that they would tell you that they really do enjoy their jobs. It is a great feeling to help someone who is hurt or scared, and detectives and other police officers and deputies take pride in keeping their communities safe. If you want to become a police officer, deputy, or detective, I would recommend that you work hard in school. Read about police officers in good books from the library. Talk to a police officer or deputy about his or her job. Try to stay in good shape physically, which includes using your common sense to avoid illegal drugs and other foolish behavior. Look for opportunities in your own life to help others who may be hurting or afraid—this is a wonderful habit no matter what you grow up to be. And finally, the best advice I ever got when I decided to become a police officer came from my chaplain at my college. He told me I would need to be strong in faith, and he was right. I would therefore respectfully encourage you to be true to your faith, as taught by your parents or elders. Again, this is a good habit for all walks of life, not just for police.

✪✪✪✪✪✪✪✪✪✪✪✪✪✪✪✪✪✪✪✪✪✪✪✪

Agencies and the Alphabet Soup

In television shows you may have heard government and law enforcement agencies referred to as "alphabet soup." This is because every agency seems to have a different three-letter acronym to shorten its name. It can be quite confusing with all of these three-letter abbreviations being thrown around. Different areas of the government are responsible for enforcing different laws. This happens through investigations, rehabilitation, and the punishment of people who break the rules. If this is your career choice, then your number one priority will be to lead your community in crime prevention. This happens through outreach programs, community participation, and well-organized agencies. They are divided into local, state, and federal departments.

Local Law Enforcement

You see members of local law enforcement agencies at work every day. These are the officers who patrol your streets and keep your neighborhood safe. The territory is usually restricted to your city or county limits. You can easily spot these agents by their uniforms and patrol cars. They use their leadership skills every day by problem solving, inspiring others, and upholding the law. They build relationships with people in the community and work together to solve problems as a team. This tough and challenging job requires bravery and courage. Your job will be to respond to emergency situations, promote safety, and stand up for people who can't protect themselves. As a local law enforcement agent, you can work  for the city police force, county sheriff's office, transit authority police, district attorney's office, or airport police.

State Law Enforcement

Your state law enforcement agents, like sheriffs, are often elected by voters to keep the state safe. If you choose to work for the state, then you will be in charge of law enforcement on the state highways and in rural areas outside city limits. You could be put in charge of a criminal investigation and work to solve a major crime. Leadership qualities are essential when it comes to protecting citizens. You have to work as a team, make life-and-death decisions, and think of the greater good of the community. As a state law enforcement agent, you have many options for employment.

You can work for the sheriff's office, state police, highway patrol, department of corrections, environmental protection department, or the fish and wildlife department. All of these agencies are always on the lookout for people with great leadership skills.

Federal Law Enforcement

Would you like to maintain public order for the entire country? Do you think it would be cool to be employed by the Department of Justice or Homeland Security? If so, you may want to dig in and get some information about leadership opportunities within the federal government. There's no shortage of opportunities. You could work for the Department of Homeland Security, Transportation Security Administration (TSA), Secret Service, Drug Enforcement Agency (DEA), or United States Park Police. These are three of the most well-known federal law agencies:

Federal Bureau of Investigations (FBI): responsible for criminal investigations into counterterrorism, cybercrime, counterintelligence, civil rights, organized crime, violent crimes, white-collar crimes, and public corruption

United States Border Patrol: responsible for keeping our borders safe and for preventing illegal goods from being transported from other countries

United States Marshal Service: hunts down fugitives; protects judges who are threatened; transports criminals; and keeps witnesses safe before, during, and after criminals are brought to trial

Military Service

Do you feel a duty to defend your country and the rights of its people? If so, you have a lot of different options when you are

FBI (Checklist Requirements)

FBI agents are required to defend the United States against criminals and terrorists. This challenging and rewarding job only takes the best and brightest people. To qualify for this position you must

★   be at least twenty-three years old,

★   be a United States citizen,

★   have a four-year college degree,

★   have a valid driver's license,

★   have three years of work experience, and

★   complete an online FBI application.

Based on this information, the FBI will decide whether or not to move someone to the next phase of the hiring process, which is testing. This involves various written tests along with an interview. Candidates who pass these tests are given a Conditional Letter of Appointment, which guarantees them a job if they pass the background check and the physical fitness test. The background check includes a polygraph test, a credit and arrest check, and interviews with different people from the candidate's life. The fitness test includes a timed one-and-a-half-mile run and three-hundred-meter run, along with a push-up and sit-up requirement. When you're hunting down the bad guys, you have to be in great shape! Specialty departments within the FBI may have additional requirements for employment. A great resource for hiring requirements can be found at fbiagentedu.org.

working in the military. The US military branches are the Army, Navy, Air Force, Marine Corps, Coast Guard, National Guard, and Air National Guard. Each has recruiters you can talk with to learn more, and you can also visit military.com to get a lot of good information. To be qualified for service, you will need a high school diploma or GED, a meeting with a recruiter, a medical exam, and basic training. You can choose to be fully enlisted, which means you want to make the military your full-time profession with advancement and leadership opportunities. You can also choose to be a reserve officer, where you serve the military on a part-time basis and attend some training every year. A reserve officer typically has a career outside of the military. Signing up for the military is a huge commitment, so make sure you do your homework and talk to everyone you can before signing on the dotted line.

★★★★★★★★★★★★★★★★★

Name: Michael Palomino
Age: 22
Job (when not studying!): Reserve Officers' Training Corps (ROTC) cadet

If you are looking for a mental and physical challenge and a way to serve your country, then ROTC may be for you. Michael Palomino is in the ROTC program at the University of Central Florida, where he is learning valuable leadership skills while earning a major in business. ROTC offers many opportunities for advancement, and college scholarships are available. One thing is for sure: Michael will be able to use his leadership training from ROTC in any business opportunities he decides to pursue after he graduates from college.

Reserve Officers' Training Corps (ROTC)

Are you interested in serving and protecting your country? If so, you can get a head start by joining ROTC. You will gain valuable leadership experience while attending college. The military will pay for your education and reward you with an officer rank upon graduation. ROTC programs are offered in the US Air Force, Army, and Navy. For more information about this program and a list of participating colleges, please visit rotc.com.

Why did you join ROTC?

I come from a military family. My mother was a navy officer, my father was an air force pilot, and my grandfather was a general in the army, so it just became a natural decision to join the armed forces, and ROTC was the best option to become an officer.

What leadership skills have you learned from ROTC?

I've learned how to deal with different people who all hail from different backgrounds. Not everyone responds the same way to leadership, so you have to be adaptive in the way you lead. I've learned that getting to know your subordinates and treating them with respect is the most beneficial to achieving success.

What are some of the challenges of the program?

The program is really limited in the funding it receives. We can only do so much and participate in such scarce training opportunities that we are unable to get the best training that we could possibly get. With the drawdown and the increase in interest, it has become extremely competitive, which also limits the program, as some people can't even participate and are denied entry into the program before being able to prove themselves.

What leadership opportunities are available in ROTC?
You get to lead in multiple positions, ranging from team leaders all the way to battalion commander. You lead anywhere from four people to an entire battalion of two hundred cadets.

What advice would you give teens who are interested in ROTC?
I would recommend [they] get involved as early as possible. They need to make sure they have above a 3.0 GPA. They should also volunteer and begin building their resumé.

✪✪✪✪✪✪✪✪✪✪✪✪✪✪✪✪✪✪✪✪✪✪✪✪

Get Educated

With so many different law enforcement agencies and jobs, it's important to know what type of education and training options you have, so you can go after the job you want. Many entry-level jobs require you to be eighteen years old and complete a twelve-to-fourteen-week police academy training program. If you are interested in moving up in the ranks or taking on a leadership role then, you will want to consider one of the following programs.

Associate of Science Degree (AS) in Criminal Justice
A two-year associate's degree in law enforcement will prepare you for entry-level careers in police agencies and border patrol. You will learn about interrogation, criminal justice, and administration.

Bachelor of Science Degree (BS) in Criminal Justice

If you're interested in exploring the many law enforcement opportunities and newest law enforcement technology, then you should consider getting a four-year undergraduate degree. You'll explore advanced topics like security administration, juvenile justice, and evidence processing. Having an undergraduate degree will give you a leg up when it comes to getting hired to and then promoted within your agency.

Master of Science Degree (MS) in Criminal Justice

This program opens the door to you being considered an expert in your area in criminal justice. This scientific program is research based and digs deeper into the nature of crime, counseling, and administration. To get into this program, you must have a bachelor's degree. Many people choose to complete this degree part-time while they are working in the law enforcement field.

> We have an incredible warrior class in this country—
> people in law enforcement, intelligence—and I thank
> God every night we have them standing fast to
> protect us from the tremendous amount of
> evil that exists in the world.[1]
>
> —BRAD THOR, BESTSELLING AUTHOR

Youth Programs in Law Enforcement

Opportunities to learn about law enforcement are everywhere. Every agency needs great people just like you, so many of them offer youth programs where you can receive on-the-job training.

Your local agencies may offer ride-alongs, teen court, the Police Athletic League (PAL), or the Police Explorer program. If you're looking for more extensive training, then you may want to consider these other programs as well.

CIA Student Internship Program

If you know you want to work for the CIA and want to get a head start on your career, then this may be the internship for you. The

application process for this program begins your senior year of high school after you've chosen to enroll in a four-year college program. As an intern, you will attend work sessions related to your college major during your summer breaks. You will receive a salary and medical and retirement benefits. In addition, the CIA

pays for your school tuition, books, and fees. The scholarship program requires its recipients to continue working for the CIA after graduation for one and a half times the length of the program, or six years. More information about this program can be found at cia.gov.

FBI National Academy Association, Inc. (FBINAA)

Every summer the FBINAA hosts a Youth Leadership Program for high school students to learn about criminal justice, the court system, and law enforcement responsibilities. To qualify, you must be between the ages of fourteen and sixteen, have good grades, and be elected by one of the forty-eight FBI chapter offices. Tuition and board for this camp is free. For more information, go to fbinaa.org.

National Student Leadership Conference (NSLC)

Would you like to experience college life, develop leadership skills, and use career simulators? If so, you may want to take a look at the NSLC summer programs. These programs offered to high school students teach team building, decision making, goal setting, and public speaking. Leadership programs in law enforcement include national security, law and advocacy, public policy, and forensic science. Additional programs in education, engineering, health, and sports management are also available. For more information, check out nslcleaders.org.

You Are Never Too Young to Be a Hero

You don't have to work in law enforcement or be super brave or strong to be a hero. Anyone can be a hero in their life, no matter how young or old they may be. Heroes help someone in a time of need, or stand up for something or someone they believe in. They are true assets to their communities and the people around them. Start working on these key heroic qualities and you'll be well on your way to making a difference in someone else's life.

★ **Appreciate the differences in other people.** Everyone has different backgrounds and perspectives, so take the time to understand the people around you. By doing this you will be able to understand how you can help. For example, if a student is being teased for wearing clothes based on a different culture, then you can diffuse the situation by reminding others to treat people how they want to be treated.

★ **Learn to resolve conflicts while showing respect to everyone.** It's easy to step into an argument and quickly take sides, while it takes time to listen to everyone's perspective. The key to solving a problem is to come to a long-lasting agreement without anyone getting angry or offended. For example, some of the members of your school club want to use the club dues to support a charity, while others would like to use them to create a website. At first you think the money should go to charity, but after listening you realize a website would be a great way to raise awareness for the charity and create fundraisers. Based on this information, both sides realize they can both reach their goals by first setting up a website.

★ **Understand the 3 Rs—Rights, Respect, and Responsibility.** Everyone should be able to be in his or her neighborhood or at school and feel safe, unhurt, and free from bullies. You can model good behavior by respecting people's rights and acting responsibly when you're out in the community. For example, some of your friends at the park think it's funny to take bikes away from the younger kids and tease them by riding around on them. You tell your friends to cut it out and redirect them to go play basketball instead.

★ **Learn to overcome obstacles.** No one has things go perfectly for him or her at all times. Sometimes obstacles are big, like growing up with not enough food to eat, and other times they are short-term, like not understanding your homework for math class. Either way you have the choice to find a solution or get overwhelmed by the problem. For example, your dad loses his job and can't afford your soccer fees. You can quit the team, or you can come up with ways to earn the money yourself so you can stay on the team you love.

★✪✪✪✪✪✪✪✪✪✪✪✪✪✪✪

Name: CIA recruitment officials
Organization: Central Intelligence Agency

Are you good at keeping secrets? Do you want a job that prevents terrorism and helps keep our nation safe? If so, you may want to consider a job with the CIA. The CIA collects, analyzes, and provides information regarding national security to the United States federal government. They have employees located all over the world who speak various languages and possess many different skills. The following is what makes a good CIA official and why you may want to look into a job with the CIA.

Describe the CIA's mission.
The CIA's primary mission is to support US policymakers by preempting threats and furthering US national security objectives by collecting foreign intelligence, producing objective all-source analysis, conducting effective covert action as directed by the president, and safeguarding the secrets that help keep our nation safe. We also develop innovative technology to meet our specialized operational needs, and we work in close collaboration with the other intelligence community members, such as the National Security Agency and the National Geospatial Intelligence Agency, to safeguard our country.

Why should someone interested in being a leader consider a career with the CIA?
The CIA has boundless career opportunities that mirror in some respects those found in many private-sector corporations. The uniqueness and importance of our foreign intelligence mission sets it apart from typical corporations because it provides support to US policymakers and helps keep our country safe from those who seek to harm the US, its interests, and its citizens. CIA careers allow individuals to work on and solve interesting, hard, unique problems and technology challenges in service to our country, which is incredibly personally rewarding. There are numerous formal and informal leadership opportunities within our organization given the depth and breadth of our mission and the ability of individuals to undertake diverse jobs across the agency. We strive to develop exceptional leaders and, consequently, we are a big proponent of continuous education and mentoring to allow our employees to expand their existing skill sets. We have created an environment where we

can lead and have multiple careers within one organization, becoming well-rounded intelligence officers who are better able to address mission challenges through the incorporation of all of our diverse experiences and perspectives.

What leadership qualities are important for CIA employees to have?

Leadership qualities are very important for CIA officers. We feel it is essential that our employees have the following qualities in order to be effective leaders in our organization: honesty, integrity, ethical behavior, courage, accountability, intelligence, creativity, resilience, open-mindedness, continuous learner, critical thinker, strong communication skills.

Furthermore, we expect our officers to respect and leverage diversity in all its forms and put the need of the team and mission ahead of personal gain. They also possess a well-defined sense of mission, purpose, values, and goals, and they are able to both lead and follow according to the situation at hand.

What student opportunities are available for someone interested in the CIA?

The CIA has a number of paid student internship opportunities for almost every career discipline at the undergraduate and graduate college levels, which include scholarships, traditional internships, and co-op programs. These internships offer students a great opportunity to undertake substantive work in their chosen career field while helping protect our country. Our students also learn about the CIA's overall mission, the mission of the various directorates that comprise the CIA, the CIA's role within  the intelligence community, and the importance of partnering with other intelligence agencies to accomplish everyone's mission goals. Additionally, students have the opportunity to participate in mentoring, shadowing, and networking opportunities, which helps them develop professionally and helps them form professional and personal bonds they can continuously leverage throughout their careers.

Teens should seek opportunities with the agency early in their career decision–making process through our paid student internships. This experience will help them determine whether a career with the CIA fits into their overall career goals. There are a variety of internships available for students during their senior year of high school, or as college undergraduate/graduate students. These internships provide students with the opportunity to undertake meaningful work to advance the agency's mission and impact US policy; they are not "grab us coffee" internships.

In regards to the application, fully complete and submit one application within the three-day application window, as all the information included will be lost after that timeframe; answer all the questions on the application, and if a question does not apply, insert that notation as the answer. Students can apply for up to four positions [for] which they feel they qualify. It is recommended the applicant prints the completed application before it is submitted as it is not accessible or editable afterward. It is advisable that the student keeps a copy of the completed application to assist in the future if one chooses to apply again as the initial information submitted will just need to be updated.

Individuals should properly prepare for the interview if they are contacted for a student or full-time employment opportunity so they can skillfully and knowledgeably respond to the questions by properly conveying their strengths and experiences to help form a good first impression. Teens should be confident in who they are and what they know. They should stay open-minded and not let new things or experiences frighten them or make them feel inadequate because student opportunities are unique learning experiences which help them grow personally and professionally. We will provide students who come on board with the guidance, education, and experiences they need as new employees to enable their success and help them learn the organization's mission and culture since the CIA is like and unlike its movie and television portrayals. In return, there is an expectation that students will perform and contribute to the mission to their fullest ability in an inclusive and collaborative manner.

Lastly, students should not become completely discouraged if they do not hear back within the initial 90 days after applying. It takes time to review the thousands of student internship applications and hundreds of thousands of full-time employment applications the CIA receives each year. Apply again if a response is not received in a year.

CIA student internships are available throughout the year. Teens can educate themselves about the various CIA student internship opportunities, specific jobs, qualification requirements, and application deadlines by visiting www.cia.gov /careers/students-opportunties.

What is the CIA looking for in candidates?
The CIA is looking for a diverse, creative cadre of intelligent and resilient individuals interested in world events and who possess integrity; a strong work ethic; expertise in their career field; leadership, critical thinking, and communication skills (both oral and written); and the ability to work in a collaborative team environment both domestically and overseas to protect our country, allies, and interests; foreign language proficiency is a plus. Additionally, we are searching for responsible individuals with good people skills that can adapt to new challenges and have an open mind to the perspectives of others. We seek those who take different problem-solving approaches and can implement the chosen solution in a professional, effective, and timely manner. We want people who are confident in their professional abilities and are comfortable speaking up about their recommendations or concerns. Moreover, we are looking for people who are curious and are always seeking to learn new things to enhance their professional and personal skill sets to advance mission accomplishment.

What advice would you give teens who are interested in a career with the CIA?

Teens interested in a career with the CIA should educate themselves about the agency's mission via our website, as well as reading the recommended intelligence literature posted on the site. It is also important to have an interest in world events, given the CIA's worldwide mission. Additionally, they should fully devote themselves to their studies and get involved in activities that help them develop leadership, critical thinking, and communication skills, including having a CIA internship, and demonstrate excellence in a chosen career field; proficiency or ability in a foreign language is also helpful. Teens should also stay away from activities that may call into question their suitability for employment (e.g., drug use, intellectual property theft, and binge drinking).

✪✪✪✪✪✪✪✪✪✪✪✪✪✪✪✪✪✪✪✪✪✪✪✪

4

Get Charitable

Do you have a cause you believe in? Are you passionate about helping others and giving back to your community? Would you like to meet interesting people while doing meaningful work? If so, nonprofit organizations could use a person just like you.

Changing the world for the better may sound really rewarding, but it's really hard work too. Most nonprofit organizations work on a tight budget, so your pay may be lower than those working in corporate jobs. You will gain plenty of fundraising skills as you and your coworkers come up with new ways to raise money for your organization. Great networking skills and enthusiasm for your organization will help you to be successful in this type of job. The stakes are much higher when your work is directly related to helping other people, animals, or the environment.

There are many ways to be a leader by serving others. You can speak on behalf of your organization to people in the community who are in a position to help with donations or time. You can train new volunteers and lead by example. You can lead the business side of the organization with tasks such as hiring, accounting, training, and fundraising. You won't find a shortage of opportunities to develop your leadership skills when it comes to working for a charitable organization. Take some time to figure out what type of cause you are most passionate about.

✪✪✪✪✪✪✪✪✪✪✪✪✪✪✪✪

Name: Kate Otto
Job: Founder and director of
Everyday Ambassador

Kate Otto seemed destined to become a social-impact leader from an early age. In high school, she spent a lot of her free time helping out at a local homeless shelter for individuals who were HIV positive. As soon as she was old enough, she traveled all over the world for various volunteer organizations, helping out where she could. After graduating from New York University with a degree in international relations and a Master in Public Health (MPH) in health policy and management, she started medical school. She founded Everyday Ambassador in 2010 to promote world-changing service work where ordinary people can become extraordinary leaders for global change. To find out how you can become a leader for the cause you're most passionate about, visit her website at everydayambassador .com or check out her new book, *Everyday Ambassador: Make a Difference by Connecting in a Disconnected World*.

Describe Everyday Ambassador.
On an individual level, an everyday ambassador (EA) is anyone striving to make the world a better place, whether globally or locally, and does so with a strong focus on respectful, responsible

human connection. EAs don't think about "saving" the world, which is a term that creates an Us/Them power hierarchy between the "helper" and person "needing help." We instead phrase our service as two-way exchanges and relationships of mutual growth and respect. Whoever we might help, we receive just as much back in return. Everyday ambassadors are self-aware, flexible, and culturally sensitive.

As for the larger movement, Everyday Ambassador is a network of global citizens who believe that human connection, even in an increasingly digital world, is the key to lasting, positive social change. The way we see it, in a world where we're more digitally connected than ever before, we're all too often less humanly connected. We let social media and digital devices get in the way of real-life conversations, and we start losing our skills for interpersonal interaction. So EA has set out to create a cultural shift in the world of travel and volunteerism/service, so that good intentions are always translated into respectful social change efforts. We envision a world in which all travelers and volunteers approach the act of crossing borders—whether national, class, race, or otherwise—with attitudes of undistracted focus, empathy, patience, and humility toward diverse people they meet.

How did it get started?
I've been passionate about public service since I was a teenager, growing up in a small town in Rhode Island, which was so homogenous it often felt claustrophobic to me. I was so eager to meet people with different lives and experiences! And by the time I got to high school, I got exactly what I asked for, even though I never left my town limits. A woman in my hometown had converted her home into a homeless shelter for people living with HIV, and throughout my four years at high school, I spent many afternoons volunteering there, which meant becoming friends with people who had struggled with abuse, addiction,

poverty, and sickness—all worlds that were as foreign to me as another country. This notion of connecting across differences —and the powerful, positive influence it had on making me a more tolerant, loving and open person—stuck with me for years, an unnamed but strong and guiding presence.

The first official concept of Everyday Ambassador finally blossomed in 2010, when I was finishing a yearlong fellowship with an HIV/AIDS organization in Indonesia. By twenty-three years of age, I had already worked on short-term service projects in Ghana, Tanzania, Mexico, and Guatemala, yet my yearlong experience in Indonesia was the first time I had an experience immersive and long enough to allow for my accu-mulating lessons in global citizenship to come to fruition. So I pulled together my various travel blogs into a single website, which I called *Everyday Ambassador*, and began articulating my analyses of twenty-first century civic engagement in this online space.

As I prepared to head back to the US after that year, I grappled with my own trajectory, considering what next step could help me lead a life of service—*Should I stay abroad and serve? Did my own country need just as much help as international locales? Should I work with grassroots communities or more powerful institutions?* At the same time I was pondering the increasingly ubiquitous tech-nologies of smartphones and social media channels, and how they could both facilitate and hinder well-intentioned efforts to form meaningful human relationships across borders. I still remember at the office in Indonesia, there was a sign posted above our computers that read (English translation): "Technol-ogy is meant to bring together people who are far away, not create new distances between people who are already close."

As I began sharing these thoughts more widely, and inviting others to participate in the *Everyday Ambassador* blog, I real-ized how many people shared the sentiment of wanting to be a responsible and effective global citizen. Eager to create more helpful resources for like-minded "everyday ambassadors," I then began writing the manuscript of a book about Everyday

Ambassadorship, and after speaking at TEDxUNC [Technology, Education, & Design] in 2012, several volunteers joined me as EA staff, and our movement was born.

What leadership skills have you gained from starting this organization?

Starting Everyday Ambassador has been an incredible exercise in leadership skills development. Most powerfully, I've learned about the beauty of horizontal leadership, meaning that my team of nine volunteers never operates as a hierarchy; rather, each individual brings a unique skill set to our team and takes responsibility for a different component of our work. Although I tend to be a die-hard planner for my own tasks (imagine a color-coded Google Calendar packed to the limits), I never micromanage my teammates, which to me is disempowering. Our relationships are instead based on trust, respect, and clear communication, and these values are particularly precious to us because we work across multiple cities, often across multiple continents! Additionally, I've realized how important it is to get to know each teammate's unique passions, personal goals, and desires for impact on the world and then tailor a role to suit their vision and skills. When someone is operating in an environment of self-fulfillment, I believe it gives them the energy and positivity to give their best every day. Each of my teammates brings their own style of leadership to our team, and I believe that a key element of good leadership is appreciating and leveraging the beautiful power of a team's diversity to benefit the organization's growth and impact.

What are some of the challenges you have encountered?

Our team's main challenge with Everyday Ambassador is that we care deeply about having a positive impact on the world, as well as measuring that impact in order to assess our progress, yet the results we aspire toward are not as easily quantifiable as those of other service-driven organizations. We're not building wells, or giving out scholarships, or providing medications. Rather, we see ourselves within the fields of volunteerism, public service, and travel as the proverbial rock that disrupts the water, the inspirational force that pushes individuals to change their civic behaviors in ways that ripple onward, past our capacity for measurement. For now, we measure our impact in terms of how many people we can influence—for example, how many organizations we partner with; how many people bring EA to their classrooms, campuses, or workplaces for a workshop; how many conversations we start on social media channels; and how many people read the EA book (after it's out May 26!).

What advice would you give teens who are interested in participating in your organization?

Our arms are wide open to teens who are interested in participating in EA! Firstly, I invite you to get started by picking up the book *Everyday Ambassador: Make a Difference by Connecting in a Disconnected World* and subscribing to our Daily Blog at everydayambassador.org/blog, both of which are full of ideas, inspiration, and resources to become an Everyday Ambassador. You can also follow us on Facebook, Twitter, and Instagram. Then, you can participate in our #AmbassadorOf campaign, which asks you to post a selfie that describes your own values around human connection. Next, you can invite Everyday Ambassador to give an Everyday Ambassador Training Workshop with your class, club, or team, if you're interested in learning even more about how to apply the principles of Everyday Ambassadorship to your life. Lastly, we are always open to receiving emails of interest if you'd like to volunteer with the Everyday Ambassador team! Please contact kate@everydayambassador.org if you are interested in learning more.

What leaders do you admire?

Leaders I most admire are not the people who create followers but rather the people who create more leaders. Many of the partner organizations of Everyday Ambassador—like Thinking Beyond Borders, Global Health Corps, America's Unofficial Ambassadors—live this value by training their participants to be incredible leaders. Creating more leaders means walking your talk and living by example; your actions demonstrate your values, and your values do not waver even in the face of immense challenges. One of my personal heroes who lived this way is Nelson Mandela, and I highly recommend his autobiography, *Long Walk to Freedom*, to all teens. Even through decades of imprisonment, he never gave up his values of justice and human dignity. Even when he was finally elected as president of South Africa after the horrific era of apartheid, Mandela stood by his values of human dignity and practiced forgiveness with his former oppressors. He believed in peace and reconciliation, and he strove to act on these values even when others pressured him to stray from them. Most of us will never have the chance to take on as high level a political role as Mandela did in his lifetime; however, every single one of us has the power to live out our values in our everyday lives, and that, to me, is the measure of an admirable leader.

✪✪✪✪✪✪✪✪✪✪✪✪✪✪✪✪✪✪✪✪✪✪✪

A leader takes people where they want to go.
A great leader takes people where they don't necessarily want to go, but ought to be.[1]
—ROSALYNN CARTER, PHILANTHROPIST AND WIFE OF THE
THIRTY-NINTH UNITED STATES PRESIDENT

Ten Types of Nonprofit Organizations

Animals: These nonprofits are concerned about the welfare of animals who may be abused, endangered, or abandoned. Examples include Wildlife Conservation Society, People for the Ethical Treatment of Animals, and the National Fish and Wildlife Foundation.

Arts, Culture, and Humanities: Organizations in this category include museums and performing arts centers. Examples include the American Museum of Natural History, the Smithsonian, and the American Bard Theater Company.

Education: This large category of charities conducts information campaigns and programs and works with zoos and many schools. Examples include Public Broadcasting Service (PBS), FHI 360 (formerly Family Health International & Academy of Educational Development), and Big Brothers Big Sisters of America.

Health: Organizations in this category raise money to cure diseases, fund research, and provide healthcare to those without resources. Examples include the American Cancer Society, St. Jude Children's Research Hospital, and the American Heart Association.

Human Services: The goal of these organizations is to improve people's quality of life by meeting their human needs. Examples include Habitat for Humanity, the American National Red Cross, and the Oprah Winfrey Foundation.

International Affairs: Organizations are involved in helping people in other countries with poverty, health, and education. Examples include UNICEF, CARE USA, and Save the Children.

Literacy: This type of organization wants to ensure that everyone has an opportunity to learn to read and write. Examples include Teach for America, the New York Public Library, and Reach Out and Read.

Membership: This type of organization provides benefits and information within a specific category such as career, race, nationality, or service. Examples include American Veterans, the American Federation of Teachers, and the National Writers Union.

Public Benefit: These are created to perform specific benefits for the community. Examples include Goodwill, the YMCA, and Marine Toys for Tots.

Just One Chocolate Bar at a Time

Do you think you're too young to make a difference? Try telling that to eight-year-old Dylan Siegel, who at age six wrote the book *Chocolate Bar* in order to raise money for his best friend, Jonah Pournazarian, who was diagnosed with a rare liver condition called GSD type 1b. He has sold his book in over sixty countries and raised over $1 million to help fund research. Dylan and Jonah have appeared on the *Today Show*, *Fox News*, *ABC News*, *NBC Nightly News*, and various other programs. For more information about *Chocolate Bar* and how you can help, visit chocolatebarbook.com.

Religious: Churches and faith-based organizations provide spiritual guidance and services to assist people. Examples include Catholic Charities USA, the YMCA, and United Jewish Communities.

citizens

Bill & Melinda Gates Foundation

If you were the founder of the largest software company in the world, how would you spend your time and money? Would you buy a yacht and travel the world? Buy houses for yourself and your family members? Throw elaborate parties and invite all your famous friends? If you're Bill Gates, then you figure out a way to give it all away.

In 1975, Bill Gates founded Microsoft Corporation, which quickly offered the most dominant computer operating system in the world. In 1995, he landed on *Forbes* magazine's "World's Wealthiest People" list and has been on that list ever since. He and his wife founded the Bill & Melinda Gates Foundation in 2000 to improve healthcare while decreasing poverty around the world and to improve education in America. Despite all of his contributions to advancing technology with Microsoft, he decided in 2006 to split his time between his company and his foundation.

He feels his biggest contribution to society is not his software success but his Giving Pledge initiative. By signing this pledge, the richest people in the world are committing to give half of their wealth to charity. "It's the most fulfilling thing we've ever done," Gates told interviewer Chris Anderson, according to the *TED Blog*. "You can't take it with you. If it's not good for your kids, let's get together and brainstorm what can be done. Part of the reason I'm so optimistic is I think philanthropy is going to grow and work on things government is just not good at shining a light on."[2]

Leading by example has worked, because now he has over 120 signatures on his Giving Pledge. His pledge has been signed by people like Warren Buffett, Mark Zuckerberg, Ted Turner, Richard Branson, and George Lucas. By starting this pledge, Bill Gates has changed the way people view charitable giving and how they can use their financial success to impact the world.

⭐⭐⭐⭐⭐⭐⭐⭐⭐⭐⭐⭐⭐⭐⭐⭐

Name: Amanda Harris
Age: 20
Job (when not studying!): Founder
of Wear Then Share

What do you do if you're in seventh grade and have a closet full of old dance costumes? Take them to Goodwill? Let them collect dust? If you're Amanda Harris, you build an organization around it. By placing collection baskets in several dance studios, religious organizations, and dance stores, she was able to gather over ten thousand dance items for kids who can't afford to buy dance costumes. She took it one step further by creating a program where kids can take dance classes for free. In 2014, her work was honored when she received a Diller Teen *Tikkun Olam* Award for $36,000. She is now a junior at Washington University in St. Louis, majoring in anthropology, with a focus on global health and the environment, with a minor in chemistry. Before she left for college, she made sure her Wear Then Share program was sustainable by training another student to help out locally, while she maintains the website, connects with people across the country to start their own Wear Then Share programs, and keeps in contact with her donors.

Describe your company, Wear Then Share.

I started the organization Wear Then Share to brighten the lives of at-risk youth through dance. Wear Then Share has two branches: a dancewear initiative, which has donated over ten thousand dance items (valued at $100,000), and a dance outreach program, which has provided regular dance classes and recitals to hundreds of students at the Boys & Girls Clubs (BGC) and the Mary Hall Freedom House.

The dance clothing that Wear Then Share recycles would otherwise be thrown out. Instead, it is given to kids who could not afford it on their own. When children who have close to nothing receive glittery tutus, their eyes light up, not to mention their parents'. While dancing is the focus of the outreach program, the organization teaches a lot more than just dance moves. Kids learn the importance of leading healthy, active lifestyles as well as life skills, such as persistence, confidence, and motivation. I feel blessed to help facilitate this journey.

How did it get started?

I express my heart, body, and soul through dance. Whether on stage in a glitzy costume or alone in a small studio, I escape into another world when I dance. I feel beautiful. Sharing my love for dance is one of the greatest gifts I can give because dance has brought me indescribable joy and has motivated me to continually try my best; I want others to experience this gift.

I started the organization Wear Then Share to enrich the lives of at-risk youth through dance. The program has reached thousands with free dancewear and has taught hundreds of talented students. Over the past seven years, I have spent over one thousand hours developing and volunteering through Wear Then Share.

I had the idea to create Wear Then Share in eighth grade after a costume fitting. I saw my fellow dance students throwing away their perfectly good, outgrown leotards, ballet slippers, and tights. My costumes, too, were piling up in my closet and accumulating dust. I knew there had to be a better use for this dancewear. I started researching organizations that donated dancewear, but none existed in Atlanta. I decided to create my own.

I called the director of Foster Care and she led me to Moving in the Spirit, which is an organization that uses dance to mentor underprivileged kids. I contacted the manager and learned about the organization's needs.

I spent a long time creating an attractive and eye-catching collection bin. My dance studio, Studio Atlanta Dance, supported the idea by allowing me to place a basket in the studio and to email every dancer. The bin flooded with donations after only a week, so I took this model to eight other locations. I met with managers of dance studios, dance stores, and churches to ask permission to set up a donation site. We discussed the logistics of the program: the pickup and delivery system, marketing, and recipients. I created a website and my own logo to put on posters, pamphlets, and flyers. I collected, washed, cleaned, sorted, and then delivered the dancewear to various organizations. Some locations embraced the idea with open arms, while others flat-out rejected it. Perhaps they struggled trusting a teenager to run an effective program. Nevertheless, I kept asking until I set up collection bins in all of the major surrounding areas of Atlanta. Wear Then Share has expanded nationwide, and people from all over the country have set up their own branches of Wear Then Share.

After a few months focusing on collecting dancewear, I wanted to do more to spread the joy of dance. Therefore, I added a dance outreach program to Wear Then Share. I contacted the director of the Boys & Girls Clubs (BGC) and set up a dance program. For six years, I taught a weekly jazz class to twenty-five students (ages six to nine) at BGC, and for three years, I arranged for my class to perform at my high school's spring dance concert. My peers loved helping out backstage with the kids. I created a club at my school to continue Wear Then Share's work and ensure the sustainability of the organization.

I also created a dance program and a costume close at the Mary Hall Freedom House, a residential homeless shelter for women and children. For two years, I taught the dance group several weeklong workshops. I also choreographed and arranged for my students to perform at the annual Christmas celebration.

How do you manage college and running your own company at the same time?

I am able to manage running Wear Then Share while in college with a lot of help! It is far from being a one-woman show. Amazing volunteers teach dance classes in Atlanta, and my mother graciously took over the dancewear initiative when I left for college. I still manage the website, stay in contact with the studios and dance stores that have collection bins, and communicate with partner organizations; however, I am only one piece of the puzzle.

During my senior year of high school, I took many steps to ensure that Wear Then Share could not only survive when I moved but would thrive. I worked closely with a peer named Margaret Wilson and trained her to lead the dance outreach program at the Boys & Girls Clubs and maintain the relationship with Westminster High School. She trained the next leader, Remi Matthews, to take over when she graduated this spring. My hope is for students to continue passing the torch and for Wear Then Share to remain a successful program.

What do you think makes a strong leader?

I believe there is no one checklist that makes a good leader; rather, anyone is capable of leadership with passion, self-awareness, and some practice. With that said, some traits certainly help!

I think compassion for others is most essential. Being able to listen to, respect, and encourage your team helps to make the work most productive, and not to mention, fun. This compassion will translate into humility and allow you to constantly improve upon yourself, your team, and your project.

Along with compassion, confidence is key. Leaders must trust their ability to lead and make decisions. It is important to note that confidence comes in all shapes and sizes. Confident leaders might be loud and engaging, or they might take a backseat and facilitate a space for all ideas to be shared and appreciated. Whatever your leadership style, confidence inspires other people to trust you and to follow you.

What skills can students start developing now to become leaders in the future?

Figure out what you believe in. What issues make your heart swell and your pulse quicken? What pains you? What excites you? Passion makes effective leaders because it keeps them motivated and invigorates their teams. In addition, discover what values drive you. Who do you want to be? These values will influence what type of leader you are.

Learn your own strengths and weaknesses. We all have both, and self-awareness helps us improve as leaders. Use this knowledge to push yourself out of your comfort zone. For example, if you know that you talk too much in a group, be aware and create room for other voices. If you find yourself taking a backseat, push yourself to contribute more. Do not let weaknesses become excuses but, rather, areas for growth.

Never, never, never give up because you are young. I cannot tell you how many times people underestimated my project's value because of my age. If you have an idea and see a need in the community, follow through and believe in yourself to make a difference.

What current or past leaders have inspired you and why?
Dr. Helene Gayle from the organization CARE is an inspiration. One story in particular epitomizes why I look up to her. Someone wanted to donate millions of dollars worth of wheat to a small, poor village. Instead of blindly accepting this generous donation, she talked to the people who would benefit from it. She came to understand how the flood of wheat would weaken the local market and devastate the lives of farmers. By listening to and understanding the community she was working with, she was better able to serve as a leader. I take this lesson to heart. We must learn from the people we are working with in order for the service we are leading to be beneficial. We must approach every situation as a learning opportunity, staying humble and flexible.

What advice would you give students who are looking to gain leadership experience right now?
Go for it; don't wait. I think it can be tempting to fall into the mind-set of waiting until you grow up in order to start doing something "important." Don't let this happen, because even kids can make a tremendous impact in their communities. Yes, kids are our future, but they are also our present.

✪✪✪✪✪✪✪✪✪✪✪✪✪✪✪✪✪✪✪✪✪✪✪✪

Where Can You Volunteer?

There are so many different places that would love your help! Here's a list that will help you get started.

Dorot: Enhance the life of elderly people by teaching computer basics, delivering birthday packages, and visiting seniors in their homes. For more information, visit dorotusa.org.

St. Jude Children's Research Hospital

Danny Thomas was living paycheck to paycheck as an entertainer when he put his last seven dollars in a church collection box. He had a baby on the way and no way to pay the hospital bills, so he prayed for help. He promised St. Jude Thaddeus, the saint of hopeless causes, that he would build him a shrine if he helped Thomas with his career. This turned out to be a prayer that would change his life forever. His career eventually took off, and he made good on his promise. After extensive fundraising efforts he opened St. Jude Children's Research Hospital on February 4, 1962.

Not only has St. Jude improved the survival rate for children with cancer and life-threatening diseases, but it has lived up to its pledge to "treat children regardless of race, color, creed or their family's ability to pay."[3] With a daily operating cost of $2 million, St. Jude relies on donations to cover its expenses. Thousands of businesses, celebrities, and organizations participate in fundraising efforts. Danny Thomas never forgot the days when he couldn't pay a hospital bill, which is why parents never receive a bill for bringing their child to St. Jude for treatment. The charity covers travel expenses, meals, lodging, and all medical charges. Thomas's vision created a place where every parent has equal access to the best medical research and technology in the world for their child. Through strong leadership St. Jude Children's Research Hospital has helped increase the child cancer survival rate from 20 percent to over 80 percent, and growing! To get more information about this amazing hospital visit stjude.org.

Do Something: Join 2.5 million people dedicated toward making the world a better place. Whether you have fifteen minutes or fifteen years to spare, they have a social campaign for you. For more information, visit dosomething.org.

Knit for Kids: Did you know you can help kids while watching television or listening to music? You can with this organization by knitting sweaters for the World Vision organization. You will be providing warmth and comfort to a child living in poverty. For more information, see knitforkids.org.

Projects Abroad: If you are between the ages of sixteen and nineteen and would like to spend part of your summer helping people in another country, then consider applying to this high school program. Project Abroad has many different locations and opportunities available. For more information, see projects-abroad.org.

Teen Life: Are you having trouble finding the right volunteer opportunity? Then visit this site to search hundreds of different options, teenlife.com.

US Department of Veterans Affairs: If you think a health services career is in your future, then you may want to check out the available opportunities at your local VA medical center. They can always use help in patient services, therapy, research, and administration. Learn more at volunteer.va.gov.

The YMCA: Girls and boys in grades seven through twelve can join the Leaders Club, which gets you involved with your community, teaches leadership skills, and helps you to develop friendships with people outside your school. There's more information at ymca.net.

Name: Morgan Davidson
Age: 16
Job (when not studying!): Founder
of the Ambassadors for Hope Club

When Morgan Davidson was just twelve years old, she made a promise to her grandmother, who was dying from cancer, that she would go out and help others battling cancer. Morgan made good on that promise and launched the Ambassadors for Hope Club. In four years she has raised over $45,000 for the City of Hope National Medical Center for Research. She has gotten people registered as bone marrow donors, founded two high school chapters of the Ambassadors for Hope Club, and donated money to the City of Hope Blood Donor Center. In 2014, she won a Diller Teen *Tikkun Olam* Award for her "lifesaver" work for the City of Hope and her leadership work in creating the Ambassadors for Hope Clubs. At just sixteen years old, she's already developed great leadership skills in fundraising and social activism.

Describe the Ambassadors for Hope Club.
I founded Ambassadors for Hope Club when I was fourteen. Ambassadors for Hope is dedicated to inspiring teens to help save lives. Our events create community involvement to help raise funds, [interest in donating] blood, and awareness for the City of Hope Blood Donor Center as well as recruit potential stem cell and bone marrow donors for Be the Match, the national stem cell and bone marrow registry. To date, we have raised $45,000-plus for the City of Hope. I took it upon myself to seek out the education needed to become an official volunteer recruiter for Be the Match, and since then, we are responsible for three hundred

people joining the registry. My leadership includes assembling several blood drives that have supplied enough blood to all the patients in need at the City of Hope for more than a week. The entirety of the project has promoted awareness to my community and inspired me to create the Ambassadors for Hope Club at two different high schools.

How did it get started?

In 2009, my grandmother was diagnosed with aggressive lymphoma. I made a promise to her that I would help as many people in her situation as possible. After she died, I held an event called Cuts for a Cure. That day we raised $29,000 and recruited twenty-five people to register for the national marrow registry. My love for giving back continued from there, and Ambassadors for Hope was born.

What leadership skills have you learned from starting your own organization?

I have learned to be organized, how to delegate, and how to multitask. I have actively pursued involving my community and have mastered how to stay hopeful in stressful situations.

What positive things have you gained by being a community service leader?

Once I began to give back, the feeling of giving hope to someone else's life was irresistible. Because of my grandmother, I feel responsible to carry out the mission and motivate other teens to get involved and help along the way. I love every minute of it, and I am excited every day to hear about the lives I have helped to save and the differences I have made at the City of Hope and Be the Match. Being a leader has opened countless doors for my future. I have been recognized with the following awards—each offering a monetary prize, which I have either donated to my causes or saved for my upcoming college education: Diller Teen *Tikkun Olam* Award, LEAD360

Jefferson Award Finalist, ABC7 Cool Kid, and 4GOOD Future 4GOODer Award.

What makes a strong leader in the nonprofit sector?
Being a strong fundraiser is not difficult when you are passionate about your mission. You just have to not be afraid to ask for help.

What advice would you give your peers who are looking to gain leadership experience now?
Find something that interests you and you feel passionate about. Build a good team to back you up, and most of all, you have to enjoy what you are doing!

Challenge
Create Your Own Campaign

Since you want to be a leader, why not try out your leadership skills with a campaign to benefit others? Toys for Tots is a great organization that collects new toys for less fortunate children and distributes them at Christmastime. You can start a collection campaign at your school or talk to your neighbors about donating toys. Everybody loves participating in a worthwhile cause.

If you like throwing parties, then throw a pajama party to gather pajamas for kids in foster care and in homeless shelters. Every person who attends your party must wear pajamas and bring at least one pair of new pajamas for donation. Hand out prizes for people who bring the most pajamas and who recruit other people to participate. You can get a lot of ideas about this type of party on the internet, so start doing your research.

Nearly everyone has canned goods in their pantries they may never use. A good way to put them to use is to donate them to a food pantry or a homeless shelter. Hand out flyers with empty grocery sacks to your neighbors for food donations and pick up their donations on a given date. Consider hosting a student car wash or fundraiser to gather money to buy food in bulk from a discount food club to round out the donation.

Starting a fundraiser is a lot of fun. Grab your friends or organize a club at school to work toward a common goal. At GenerationOn.org, you can download information on how to start your own service club. By starting your own club you will make friends, have fun, and help other people in the process. What else could a leader ask for? Warning: helping others can become addictive!

5

Get Educated

When you think of being a leader in education, do you think of spending even more time in school—as a principal, dean, or administrator—and find yourself dreaming of summer vacation? Those are great jobs for a lot of people, but if you'd like to work outside the school, you have a lot of options too. As an educational advocate you can represent students and parents to insure that every child gets the best education possible based on their individual needs. Or a lobby group where you work with a group of people to influence congress to vote a certain way on educational issues. As a policy changer you have the opportunity to pass laws and make new rules for schools. These leadership positions may put you in charge of hiring teachers, building teams, preparing budgets, making school rules, choosing curriculums, and assessing standardized testing. The only requirement is for you to have the desire to improve educational systems.

Become a Scout

Boy Scouts of America and Girl Scouts of the USA give kids of all ages opportunities to gain independence, build character, work as a team, and learn leadership skills. Activities include monthly meetings, camping, and public service projects. An important part of both organizations is earning merit badges based on completing new activities or learning new skills. If this sounds interesting to you, then check out the Boy Scouts at scouting.org or the Girl Scouts at girlscouts.org.

SPOTLIGHT

Malala Yousafzai

We've all had those days when we woke up and thought, "I wish I didn't have to go to school today," but we'd never want to lose our opportunity to get an education. What if going to school wasn't an option? This is what happened to Malala Yousafzai in 2007 when the Taliban invaded her town in Pakistan and told her that girls were no longer allowed to attend school. She was just ten years old. By age eleven, she had given her first speech, titled "How Dare the Taliban Take Away My Basic Right to Education?" After all of the girls' schools in her hometown were shut down, she began blogging about her daily life under the alias Gul Makai. She used an alias because speaking out against the government put her and her family's lives in danger.

By 2009, she was being interviewed on a regular basis about the school shutdowns. She appeared in the documentaries *Class Dismissed* and *A Schoolgirl's Odyssey* before being identified as the blogger Gul Makai. In 2011, she was nominated for Desmond Tutu's International Children's Peace Prize and Pakistan's first National Youth Peace Prize. In 2012, she was shot in the head by Taliban gunmen and survived the attack.

Protests across the world demanded that girls in Pakistan be given the right to an education. Pakistan's president, Asif Ali Zardari, launched an education fund in 2012 in Malala's honor, and girls returned to school. Malala has been nominated for the Nobel Peace Prize, won the United Nations Human Rights Prize, and was named to *Time* magazine's "Most Influential People of 2013" list. She published her story in a memoir titled *I Am Malala: The Girl Who Stood Up for Education and Was Shot by the Taliban*. Her strong belief in educational equality and her strength to deliver that message fueled a movement that will benefit girls everywhere.

What's Your Theory?

In education, four types of leadership are the most common. They are transformational, distributed, strategic, and instructional. There's no right or wrong answer when it comes to choosing a leadership style. You have to pick the one that best fits your personality and your organization.

Transformational Leadership: If you know how to inspire other people and motivate them to do great things, then you have a gift when it comes to working with people. You can communicate the changes you want to take place and let other people use their creativity to make them happen. For example, you may suggest a fundraiser, but let your staff organize it based on their interests and talents.

Distributed Leadership: If you're good at identifying other people's talents, then you should consider sharing the responsibility for obtaining your organization's goals. This builds cooperation and encourages specialties. For example, for your school fundraiser, you may put the art department in charge of decorations, while the business department focuses on the budget.

Strategic Leadership: If you spot strengths and weaknesses in  an organization and use them to your group's advantage, then you're a strategic thinker. You can see where you want to go and find a way to get there. For example, you want to put a new computer lab in your school but don't have the money for it. You know you have a lot of parent and student involvement, so you decide to have a school fundraiser.

Instructional Leadership: This is the leadership style to pick if student learning is your number one focus. You set academic goals, obtain the necessary resources, and create improved learning opportunities for the students. For example, you want to raise students' scores on the SAT standardized test, so you set schoolwide test score goals, purchase SAT prep software, and schedule time for students to learn test-taking strategies.

⊛⊛⊛⊛⊛⊛⊛⊛⊛⊛⊛⊛⊛⊛⊛⊛⊛

Name: Bonnie Guertin
Job: Executive director of Lutz
Preparatory School

Bonnie Guertin has a big responsibility
on her hands. She must find a way to make
students, teachers, and parents happy about education. This all has to occur as her school strives to make high
scores on standardized tests and prepare students for higher
education. She comes well prepared, with over twenty years
of educational experience. She has an undergraduate degree
in special education and a master's degree in education leadership. Her leadership style is team focused, so everyone helps
contribute to the school's success.

How did you get started in education?
From an early age, I knew that I wanted to work in education,
even though I tried a few other majors when I got to college.
The course of studies I undertook did not appeal to me. Long
story short, I returned to education because it ignited a passion
in me.

What made you want to move from teaching to leader-ship?
I loved being a classroom teacher, enamored with the perceived
favorable impact unfolding before me. A series of unexpected
events in my life challenged my original belief
that being a classroom teacher was the only
course that could create a positive change in
a school setting. Many of the skills I utilized
as a classroom educator have transferred very
successfully to leadership.

What are some of the challenges educational leaders face?

There are many challenges facing school leaders today. Two that are impactful are children in poverty and state mandates.

Educating students who live in poverty is an immense challenge. Some of the parents who live in poverty do not have the flexibility to be highly involved in their children's school due to their life circumstances. Parent involvement in a child's education is linked strongly to academic success.

Motivating and encouraging teachers and staff when state mandates impact the classroom learning environment is an important task. A positive school climate is critical for a happy and healthy staff even when there are various opinions. State mandates can place unexpected burdens on teachers, yet when sustained by encouragement and guidance from leadership, teachers can produce favorable outcomes.

What do you think makes a strong leader?

A strong leader isn't afraid to admit they don't have all the answers. I also think it's very important to admit when you are wrong. A strong leader shows compassion and cares for their staff when they experience hardship or crisis. A strong leader gains concurrency from staff so that leadership and teachers can share a common vision. A strong leader focuses on data for instructional purposes but not over common sense. A leader needs to set goals and monitor progress throughout the year, hand in hand with teachers and staff.

What skills can students start to develop now to become leaders in the future?

Sharpening listening skills, being a team player, learning to prioritize tasks, remembering to keep an open mind, and honing the ability to see the bigger picture are just a few traits that can build a strong foundation as a leader.

What advice would you give students who are looking to gain leadership experience?

Volunteering for leadership roles is a great avenue to gaining experience. A mentor of mine gave me some great advice once: "In leadership you need to develop the hide of a rhino and yet keep the heart of a butterfly."

✪✪✪✪✪✪✪✪✪✪✪✪✪✪✪✪✪✪✪✪✪✪✪

Ninety percent of leadership is the ability to communicate something people want.[1]
—DIANNE FEINSTEIN, CALIFORNIA STATE SENATOR

SPOTLIGHT

Alia Sabur

At the age of 18, Alia Sabur entered the Guinness World Records books for becoming the youngest full-time professor in the world. She's now 26 and working as an attorney for the US Patent and Trademark Office. Here's a look at her amazing life so far:

★ age 8 months, learns to read

★ age 5 completes elementary school

★ age 9 earns a black belt in Tae Kwon Do

★ age 10 starts college classes at State University of New York at Stony Brook

★ age 11 is considered a child prodigy as a clarinetist

★ age 14 graduates summa cum laude from college

★ age 17 receives her master's degree in materials science and engineering

- ★ age 18 becomes an international professor teaching advanced technology
- ★ age 21 enters law school at Georgetown University
- ★ currently an attorney at the US Patent and Trademark Office

Celebrities Who Earn an A+ in Educational Leadership

Andre Agassi: This tennis champ is changing educational policy for public schools through his Andre Agassi Foundation for Education. So far, they've raised over $177 million and have opened their own charter school. This allows kids of all economic backgrounds to get the education they deserve.

Derrick Brooks: Impressive on the field, this former NFL player is just as amazing off the field. Through his Derrick Brooks Charities, his mission is to provide educational opportunities, training, and inspiration to youths who are at an economic disadvantage. He opened the Brooks DeBartolo Collegiate High School in Tampa, Florida, to make a high-quality college prep education available to all youth and to show how a quality education can create opportunities.

Katherine McPhee: This singer has a special place in her heart for Burkina Faso, West Africa, which is the third-poorest country in the world. After providing mosquito nets through the Malaria No More program, she has now turned her attention toward breaking the cycle of poverty by increasing literacy. Partnered with the buildOn organization, she is paying for schools to be built.

Katy Perry: Inspiring people to "Make Roar Happen," this singer is asking people to make a one-dollar donation at Staples office supply stores to help fund classroom projects. Just recently, the campaign filled all forty-eight of the classroom project requests in Minneapolis, Minnesota.

LeBron James: We all know this NBA player can slam dunk, but did you know he has a vested interest in education in Akron, Ohio? He supports his home-town by encouraging kids to get an education and to lead healthy lifestyles. His LeBron James Family Foundation, which he runs with his mother and wife, helps students to build a community support system. 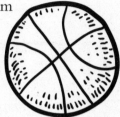 A student participating in his after-school program from third grade until high school graduation can get homework help, exposure to extracurricular activities, and skills for college.

 **Pharrell Williams:** There's more to Pharrell than musical talent and a memorable hat—he's also a big believer in education. He founded From One Hand to AnOTHER with the mission to give at-risk kids the tools they need to succeed. He uses community centers to create safe environments where kids can learn technology, art, and media.

Serena Williams: She can do more than just win every ten-nis tournament out there. She also has the Serena Williams Foundation, which provides scholarships and grants to high school students who would like to attend college, learn a trade, or start a business.

Usher: Along with his New Look charity, which focuses on leadership for young people, this singer has partnered with Scholastic Books to promote reading in the Open a World of Possible initiative.

will.i.am: This entertaining and talented singer does more than just inspire with his words. He inspires through his i.am.angel foundation, which provides mentoring and college scholarships to hardworking students who need financial assistance. His commitment to brighter futures for students motivated him to provide the funding for the Prince's Trust to teach technical and digital skills to disadvantaged youth.

Get Educated at Botangle

Someone who can take a $1,000 gift and turn it into $100,000 in less than two years is pretty impressive. When that person is still in high school, it's really unbelievable! Erik Finman, age fifteen, has taken his earnings and used them to start his newest venture, which is an online learning site. Botangle .com connects instructors with learners, so people can take control of their education. Over twenty people call Finman their boss, and he's gaining new users every day. He proves that you're never too young to be a leader and to take control of your education.

✪✪✪✪✪✪✪✪✪✪✪✪✪✪✪✪

Name: Joshua Toch
Age: 19
Job (when not studying!): Founder of Mind Before Mouth

Joshua Toch wasn't supposed to walk, let alone run, which he did when he joined his school's cross-country team. Born with cerebral palsy, Joshua has never let his disability define him. During a Rotary Club contest, he gave a speech about being bullied, and his speech made an impact. He started Mind Before Mouth and began giving speeches to small and large groups. In 2013, he was elected to attend the American Legion Boys Nation and meet President Barack Obama and was selected for the Rotary Youth Leadership Academy. The Morgan Hill, California, Chamber of Commerce chose him as its 2014 Student of the Year. His most recent accomplishment was winning a $36,000 award for visionary community service from the Helen Diller Family Foundation. In August of 2014 he will become the nineteenth member of his family to attend UC Berkeley.

Describe Mind Before Mouth.

We are a nonprofit organization that deals with bullying and self-empowerment. We go to different schools and rotary clubs and bring our stories to them. Each presenter has a different story. We tell our personal stories and get the audience to tell their stories. In a nutshell, Mind Before Mouth is a platform for all different types of people to share the stories in their hearts. It's a really moving experience, because we directly relate to the audience and say, "It's okay—you're not alone." One of the most powerful things is one of my past bullies is now one of my speakers. He talks about how he used to bully me and what changed him. It's really amazing what he does and how we can present both sides of the story.

How did it get started?

In my ninth-grade year, the Rotary Club was hosting a speech contest. I had never spoken in front of more than thirty people at one time. I knew Rotary Club had over one hundred members, but I thought, "What the heck? I'll give it a go." I spoke about camping, and my speech was less than okay, but it was a good experience. Sophomore year came, and I decided I wanted to win this time. I didn't want to just talk about camping. I was spinning my head round and round on what to talk about in my speech. The day before the competition I still had no idea what to talk about, and one of my family members told me to talk about my disability and being bullied. I said, "No way," and he said it would make a really impactful and good speech. I went in my room, closed the door, and quickly wrote the speech. I practiced it once, twice, three times. I put it away and went to bed. The next morning I got up, went to the Rotary Club, and gave my speech. During the competition, no one is allowed to make a sound until the end. After my speech, everyone was silent.

Months after I gave the speech, people were still congratulating me. I thought if my speech was still impactful after six months, then I had to do something with it. I started to speak to audiences of twenty, forty, one thousand people, and then realized I couldn't portray everyone. Then I got the idea of getting more speakers to accompany me to tell their stories. That's when Mind Before Mouth got started.

What have you learned from becoming a public speaker?
I've learned how different people are, but how similar we are too. I've spoken to middle schoolers and at elderly homes. It's amazing their different backgrounds, but everyone has something that ties them all together. After a speech, the emotional responses of people are so similar, but they come from different areas. One person might say, "I used to be a bully" or "I was bullied."

What leadership skills have you learned?
It has taught me that persistence and patience go hand in hand. Things take way longer than you would ever imagine to get done. You need to have that persistence to keep at it and the patience not to get too frustrated. To get into a school to speak, you have to go through the school, then they have to check with the district leaders, and then it goes up the chain.

Leadership is all about holding people accountable but also letting them off the hook. For example, we had a speech we had to give early in the morning, and one of my speakers slept through her alarm and missed giving her speech. She apologized. I had to convey the message that it wasn't okay, but at the same time, everyone makes mistakes. We really needed her that day, but it was just a mistake.

What makes a strong leader?
Not being in the spotlight when you don't have to be. Here's an example: There are four speakers at each speaking engagement we do. I put myself last to speak, and I introduced each speaker and talked about how amazing they were, their history and accomplishments. When it came time for me to speak, I wasn't going to introduce myself. One of my speakers grabbed the microphone and wanted to introduce me. My point was that I wanted to give them recognition for what they do because without them I'm nothing. I'm nothing. I'm my one speech, which is not as powerful as what they add.

What advice would you give students who are looking to gain leadership experience?
Look at the world and how you want to change it, and do it without stopping. Sports are great because it's team building. Another aspect is doing things out in the community. Being out and meeting people. You look at these business leaders and people around you and see what they do and how they act. Even if you're not out with your notepad taking down notes, you're still taking in how they present themselves and how they treat others. Whatever world you are immersed in, that is what you begin to act like. Make sure the people you are around are the people with the kinds of character traits you wish to have some day.

✪✪✪✪✪✪✪✪✪✪✪✪✪✪✪✪✪✪✪✪✪✪✪✪

Peace Corps

If you have an interest in living abroad and helping others, then you might want to consider applying to be a Peace Corps volunteer. This service organization has been making a difference in over 140 countries since 1961. Its goal to "promote world peace and friendship" has allowed it to help with agriculture, community economic development, education, environmental changes, health, and youth development.[2] Most volunteer needs fit into the education or health category and account for over 62 percent of the placement opportunities. If you have a bachelor's degree and can make a 26-month commitment, the following experiences might be right for you:

★ Live and work in a foreign community as a teacher to improve students' communication skills, increase literacy, develop teaching materials, and provide support for parents.

★ Raise awareness about community health issues such as clean water, sanitation, disease, and nutrition.

★ Work with local leaders to raise awareness about preventative health measures, outreach programs, and building safe water facilities.

These are just a few examples of leadership opportunities within the Peace Corps. If you visit its website, peacecorps.gov, you will have access to videos, volunteer opportunities, and questions about the application process. You can read interviews with past volunteers and see a full list of requirements. Volunteering abroad isn't for everyone, but for the right person it is a rewarding, educational, and memorable experience.

Imagine you have been put in charge of your school and are responsible for academics, school rules, and making students and parents happy. What changes would you make? You might think that shortening the day to two hours, allowing cell phones in class, and eliminating hard classes is a great start toward gaining popularity in your new position. But have you considered the consequences? If you went to school for only two hours or got rid of hard classes, then you would have a hard time passing the SAT and other standardized tests. Cell phones would be a distraction for students and teachers. Your popularity wouldn't last long if people started failing their classes and couldn't get into college.

Instead, let's consider some changes you could make to your school that would have a positive impact. For example, in Florida, many schools are starting to require students to take Spanish language class year-round. This is because of the large number of Spanish-speaking people in the state and the necessity to be able to communicate in personal and business situations. In order for schools to add this program, they must consider the cost of hiring a full-time teacher, what they will eliminate from the course schedule to free up the time in students' schedules, and how parents will feel about this decision. It takes a lot of behind-the-scenes work to make changes.

See if you can come up with not only a change you can make but how you can accomplish it. Remember to consider cost, time, resources, and parents' reactions. As a leader, you must be able to explain your vision and the positive impact it will have for others. Practice selling your idea. Warning: doing this exercise may give you a newfound respect for your school leaders and how hard it is to make changes.

6

Get Entertained

Defining *leader* can be a little tricky when you think of the entertainment industry. The first names that come to mind may be your favorite actors, musicians, or athletes. They may be the people starring in your favorite television shows or scoring points for your favorite teams, but they may not be leaders of an industry. Remember, the word *lead* means "to make rules or to direct people." This may be a team coach, television network executive, or film studio head. These behind-the-scenes people allow our favorite entertainers to do their jobs and provide infrastructure or standards for the industry. The word  *entertainment* covers a lot of ground—including circus clowns, karaoke singers, and fire-eaters—but you'll find the most jobs, and the most movers and shakers, in "the big four":

Television and Film

Directors and producers have the awesome responsibility of being in charge of production, technical, and creative teams for a film or television show. They work with the executive producer, who represents the studio and makes sure the film is finished on time and sticks to the agreed-upon budget. The marketing executive takes the finished production and leads a campaign to promote and sell the film or movie. All of these people are leaders and manage a variety of people who help them to get their jobs done.

✪✪✪✪✪✪✪✪✪✪✪✪✪✪✪✪

Name: Emily DiPrimio
Age: 14
Job (when not studying!):
Screenwriter and director of
Carver

As a fourteen-year-old, you might assume Emily DiPrimio's days are spent studying math, English, and history, not slasher films, music scores, and film production techniques. Her idea for writing a 1980s-style slasher film started when she was thirteen years old and was encouraged by her father. She launched a campaign on the fundraising website Kickstarter and raised over $31,000 from five hundred people who believed in her idea. Since then, she has shot all of the film footage, released a movie trailer, and is now working on postproduction to complete the film. *Cosmopolitan*, the *Huffington Post*, MTV, and various other media outlets have followed her story and are keeping tabs on her success. She led her cast and crew (many of them adults) in the filming process and proved that a teen can work in the film industry. She is a great example of how you can start with an idea and make it reality.

Describe your movie project.

Carver is a movie reminiscent of the '80s-style slasher films where a group of teenagers are haunted by a despicable act they committed when they were younger. Their actions caused the deaths of three innocent people. Now, on the anniversary of those deaths, an ominous calling card in the form of a carved pumpkin has been placed at each of their homes. Someone is out for revenge, the question is who.

How did the project get started?

My father and I were working on a web series called *Violet* when I began feeling constant pain in my ankle. This pain led to reconstructive surgery and had me off my feet for six to eight weeks. My father, in an attempt to relieve my depression and boredom, suggested we write a script together, which turned out to be *Carver*. After finishing the screenplay, I asked my father if we could make the film and if I could direct. He said we could if we could raise the money. So I created my Kickstarter campaign with the help of my dad and Edan Cohen (editor/producer). My campaign attracted over five hundred backers and helped me raise $31,900. After taxes, Kickstarter fees, and bounced pledges, I had a little north of $25,000, which was my original goal.

What leadership skills have you learned from directing a film?

The most important leadership skill I learned was how to deal with different personalities. Not everyone responds to the same leadership tactics, especially creative people. Learning to motivate different people with different tactics was crucial in getting *Carver* finished. It was tough the first couple of days, but once I was able to get a grasp of what motivated each person, I was able to adapt. For example, some of my actors needed constant reassurance. I always had to tell them how great they were and that they really nailed that scene. If I didn't they would wonder what they did wrong. Other actors would just know I was happy with their performances when I yelled, "Moving on."

What challenges have you faced with managing so many cast and crew members?
The biggest challenge I faced initially with managing my cast and crew members was getting them to listen to someone considerably younger. I was lucky in the fact that some of the people working on the film had worked with my father and me previously, so there was a familiarity with me. The people who were working with me for the first time seemed a little reluctant at first, because of my age and my seeming lack of experience. Once they saw I wasn't some obnoxious, entitled teenager and I knew what I was doing, it was easier for them to have a fourteen-year-old as their leader.

How do you manage school and directing/producing a film?
I filmed the movie in the summer, so I wasn't in school at the time. However, preproduction, postproduction, and promotion have all fallen during school hours. Luckily, I am homeschooled and that provides flexibility, so I can pursue my dream of being a filmmaker.

What are your three best leadership qualities?
I believe my three best leadership qualities are my passion for what I am trying to accomplish—it inspires those working with me to achieve our goals; my ability to adapt to personalities and situations; lastly, my patience. In the world of independent filmmaking the term *hurry up and wait* is often heard. If you can't quickly adapt when something bad happens or come up with fast solutions when something doesn't quite work, then independent filmmaking is not for you.

What advice would you give teens who have a great idea but are nervous about leading a project?

My advice would be it isn't as scary as you think, so go for it. Now, that doesn't mean you should go grab a camera and fly in blind. It is important that when you decide to lead a project that you have a solid plan. If you can build a solid plan on how to achieve your great idea, then the rest will fall into place. Do the research. See what others have done to achieve what you ultimately want to achieve, and follow through. Always finish what you start.

✪✪✪✪✪✪✪✪✪✪✪✪✪✪✪✪✪✪✪✪✪✪✪✪✪✪

Print and Online Media

This type of media includes newspapers, magazines, and books. The publisher is the head honcho in this business and makes major decisions including finances, hiring, and what goes into the publication. However, this isn't the only leadership role in print media. There's room for many different leadership roles in this industry. The editor-in-chief reports to the publisher and is responsible for the final product of the publication. This person often represents the publication at special events. The managing editor manages the day-to-day tasks and supervises the assistant editors and writers. Other departments, like marketing and advertising, and literary agencies also include their own leadership positions.

> Surround yourself with people who are smarter than you. Pick people who are interested in what you're interested in.[1]
>
> —RUSSELL SIMMONS, FOUNDER OF DEF JAM RECORDS

Sports

Every athletic team has a team president who is responsible for making sure the team makes money. The president is responsible for filling stadium seats, selling broadcast rights, and licensing for souvenirs. The general manager reports to the president and is in charge of developing a team that wins. A team's coach recruits new players, develops game strategies, and works with the players to improve individual and team performance. A coach may have a variety of assistant coaches to help with specialized training. Every sports team has a support staff for marketing, broadcasting, retail, and business.

What Do Athletic Coaches and Other Types of Leaders Have in Common?

You may not think athletic coaches and movie producers have a lot in common, but being a leader of any kind involves a lot of coaching skills! Whether you're planning on working on or off the field you can learn a lot from a coach. See if you can coach your way to a winning team by applying these skills to a project or organization.

Assess Your Team: Can you look at each player and see where that person is now and where he or she needs to go? Consider a person's current performance and develop a plan to reach desired performance.

Invest in Development: Just like a baseball coach has hitting and pitching coaches to help players become better on the field, you have to provide the resources for your team to improve too. Does someone need specialized training, a class, or mentorship? Your team members will work harder for you when they know you are interested in their development.

Organize Practice: A successful coach holds sporting practice on a regular schedule and is prepared. It's important to touch base with your team and to always have an agenda. People like productive meetings.

Support and Encourage: It's better to build people up than tear them down, so let your team know you are rooting for them.

Have Courage: Sometimes you have to make a tough call like finding a new position for a player or changing your strategy midgame. Be willing to take risks and try new things.

Drive Hard and Get Good Results: At the end of the day, you are responsible for your team's performance. Being a coach and leader means that you're in charge, so be willing to work hard to meet your goals.

✪✪✪✪✪✪✪✪✪✪✪✪✪✪✪✪

Name: David Eiland
Job: Pitching coach for the Kansas City Royals

Dave Eiland knows a thing or two about pressure and excitement. He's had a front-row seat to two Major League Baseball Championship World Series as a pitching coach: first, in 2009, with the New York Yankees, and most recently, in 2014, with the Kansas City Royals. He spent the first ten seasons of his baseball career as a pitcher before retiring in 2000 to begin his career as a coach. Whatever field you have an interest in leading, there's a lot to be learned from someone who's used to working with a team, like hard work, consistency, and accountability. After phenomenal recent seasons, we can't wait to see what the Kansas City Royals will do next!

What kind of leadership skills do you need to be a coach?
You have to be consistent about how you approach things every day. You have to stay calm when situations get tight. When the game gets intense, you can't show any type of panic. You have to stay under control and lead by example. Stay cool under pressure. Be accountable for your decisions and any mistakes you make and turn the page and move past them.

What personality traits have helped you most in being a coach?
Perserverance and consistency! The players have to know what they are going to get out of me every day. My job is to let them know what I expect of them on a daily basis.

How do you give feedback to players to make it productive?
I have to be honest with them. They know they are going to get constructive criticism from me. Usually when a player does something wrong as far as making a mistake (whether it's physical or mental), he knows it. I have to point it out to him anyway, so we can talk about how to avoid making that mistake  again. I touch on the mistake, but then right away start focusing on the positive: what he did right. The key is to not dwell on the bad. If I beat a player down, I'm not going to get the best out of him. It's also important to know the individual and his personality. You can't treat every player the same because they are all made up differently.

What are the challenges of being a coach in regards to working with other coaches, management, and fans?
The bottom line is that you have to produce in the area that you are in charge of. For me, the pitchers have to produce and

perform to a certain level of expectations. The biggest challenge as a coach is that you don't get to pick the players. The front office organization gives you the players, and they might be drafted players, players we traded for, or free agents we've signed. You have to get the best out of what someone else gave you. Football coach Bill Parcells said, "They want you to cook the dinner—at least they should let you shop for the groceries."[2]

The biggest challenge of a baseball coach is the grind of a long season. We play 162 games in 180 days. It's every day you are with these guys. You're on a bus with them, at the clubhouse with them, on a plane with them, in a dugout with them. You are with them seven days a week for eight to twelve hours a day. The challenge is to stay consistent even if it becomes a grind. Stick to your convictions and lead these guys to perform at their best.

What advice would you give a teen who is interested in becoming a coach?
Play the sport that you want to coach, so you have a feel for what the players are going through. Walk in their shoes first, even if it's not at the highest level, or you don't feel that you're very good or talented enough to do it. At least try to play, so you know what's happening on the other side.

✪✪✪✪✪✪✪✪✪✪✪✪✪✪✪✪✪✪✪✪✪✪✪✪

Music

Does your singing voice limit you to singing in cars and in your shower? That's no problem, because you can still have a successful career in the music industry. A record label has a variety of leadership roles for anyone who loves music. The A & R department has the fun job of discovering new talent, choosing songs, and picking music producers. A music producer takes an artist through the rehearsal and recording process to produce an album. The

promotion, marketing, and booking departments take the finished album and make sure it's played on the radio, heard in concerts, and talked about in print media. Leaders in these departments have whole teams of people who help them turn their musicians into superstars!

What's a Napoleon Complex?

Emperor Napoleon Bonaparte ruled France from 1804 to 1815 and has often been described as a tyrant and a ruler who purposely went to war to overcompensate for the fact that he was short. *Napoleon complex* has become a term associated with someone who uses mean and bossy behavior to cover up a personal deficiency.

SPOTLIGHT

Oprah Winfrey

How does a girl born in rural Mississippi into a household of poverty and abuse end up on *Time* magazine's "*Time* 100: The Most Important People of the Century" list? Is it from good luck or a fairy godmother? No! It's from hard work, determination, and grit. This media mogul, philanthropist, and producer will continue to inspire many generations of people to be their best selves, just like she did.

Oprah got her start in 1976 as a talk show host for *People Are Talking*. Some media leaders noticed her work (if you're a leader, you may discover the next

Oprah!), and soon she was in Chicago hosting a morning show called *A.M. Chicago*. During this time, she starred in Steven Spielberg's award-winning movie *The Color Purple*. Her life was never quite the same after that; her popularity soared.

In 1986, she started *The Oprah Winfrey Show*, which would change the talk show industry. Instead of talking (only) about gossip, her show focused on self-improvement, spirituality, and interviews. Her ratings skyrocketed. Books that made it into Oprah's Book Club became instant bestsellers. Once a year she hosted an "Oprah's Favorite Things" show, and the showcased items became "necessities" overnight.

Her greatest achievements can be measured by her charitable efforts. In 1998, she founded Oprah's Angel Network, which has helped build schools in underdeveloped countries, provided scholarships, and helped fight abuse. Her personal donations to educational causes exceed $400 million, and she's raised millions of dollars more through her efforts. In 2013, President Barack Obama presented her with the Presidential Medal of Freedom, which is the highest honor given to a civilian who has significantly contributed in some way to the United States.

The Oprah Winfrey Show ended in 2011, but instead of retiring, Winfrey decided to start a television network called OWN. In addition, she manages her magazine, *O: The Oprah Magazine*, that she started in 2000. Winfrey continues to be a leader in her industry and is a great example of how anyone can achieve the American Dream.

Challenge
Be an Aspiring Leader

As an aspiring leader who is hoping to make it in the entertainment industry, you must start practicing the skills used by successful leaders. This is a competitive business, and many people would love to be an entertainment leader. With a little practice and preparation, you can give yourself a leg up in becoming the ultimate entertainment leader. Read the following suggestions and see if you can make them a part of your everyday life. Practice them as often as you can, and soon you won't even have to think about doing them. They will become a part of your personality and how you communicate with other people.

Walk the Walk: Model the behavior you are trying to gain from others. Nothing is more annoying than someone who is constantly telling people to do something that person isn't willing to do. If you don't practice what you preach, then you'll have a hard time getting others to do it. For example, don't get involved in an antibullying campaign at school and then come home and tease the kid who lives across the street.

Leave Your Whine at Home: It's easy to sit back and complain about things and never offer any solutions. A real leader finds a solution and takes action to solve a problem. In the entertainment industry, you are dealing with egos, talent, and high expectations, so you have to be a problem solver. Play the what-if game to test your skills by solving the following problems: What would you do if the star quarterback broke his leg before the championship game? What would you do if the drama teacher got sick before a play's opening performance?

What if your journalism department lost funding and could no longer afford to produce a paper?

Create the Vision: As a leader, you need to present a challenge and persuade other people of its significance. People want to be involved in something they feel is important. Paint a vision, and people will feel lucky to be part of the team. For example, come up with an idea for a YouTube video series and then recruit your friends to become involved. Lead the project.

Appreciate Everyone: No matter how little or big his or her contribution, everyone likes to be recognized. Not everyone can be the star player or be the best at everything. Your job as a leader is to make everyone feel important. When you show your appreciation, people will be more willing to work hard for you. For example, you can practice this by thanking your teachers, appreciating people who help you in school or at work, and making positive comments about other people's contributions or ideas.

Their Greatest Role Yet

Your favorite entertainers may be athletes, actors, or singers. They may have originally caught your attention because of their amazing talent. Now some entertainers are giving fans another reason to appreciate them . . . by their excellent work off the stage or sports field. Many have decided to use their influence and following to bring attention to important issues. They are leading people to charitable giving, public service, environmental concern, and political involvement. Check out the following entertainers who are leading by example:

★ **Elizabeth Taylor:** This actress became a spokesperson and fundraiser in the early 1980s for HIV and AIDS, which was a little-known disease at the time. She became a founding national chairman for the American Foundation for AIDS Research (amfAR). In 1991 she increased her involvement by founding the Elizabeth Taylor AIDS Foundation, which has provided over $17 million to organizations that are working to prevent the spread of HIV. For more information visit the foundation's website at elizabethtayloraidsfoundation.org.

★ **Lady Gaga:** This performer may garner attention for her creative costumes, but her connection with her young fans has been her largest influence. These fans, called her "little monsters," inspired her to establish the Born This Way Foundation in 2012. This youth-empowering foundation provides resources for suicide prevention, bullying, body acceptance, and LGBT support. With over 13 million Instagram followers, Gaga sends a message of self-acceptance. At social media site littlemonsters.com, youths connect to share stories, network, and collaborate on creative projects.

★ **Warrick Dunn:** This former football running back for the Tampa Bay Buccaneers has received just as many awards and as much attention off the playing field. His organization, Warrick Dunn Charities, helps families and communities grow through education, economic assistance, and good nutrition. Homes for the Holidays gives people the opportunity to become first-time homeowners with financial aid, household furnishings, and education. His Betty's Hope Program provides support to youth who have lost a parent due to death, divorce, deployment, or incarceration. For more information on his many charitable projects please visit wdc.org.

7

Get Spiritual

Do you feel a spiritual calling? Maybe you have a strong belief, and you want to teach it to other people? Religion and spirituality come in many different forms for people all over the world with different beliefs. If you want to be a spiritual leader, you have a great responsibility to your followers. They will be looking to you for guidance and teachings of your shared faith. You will need to inspire, inform, and instruct people on teachings that will affect their personal and professional lives. On top of your speaking duties, you will probably be involved in building membership, raising money, and organizing service projects. When you think of a spiritual leader, you probably don't think of needing business skills, but it's important to know that almost any occupation requires you to have them. So, if you're interested in being a spiritual leader, then sign up for an accounting or public speaking class at school to round out your skills. Take every opportunity you can to read up on different religions and beliefs. Have fun—your spiritual journey awaits you!

Spiritual leaders never stop reading, studying, and increasing their knowledge in their beliefs. Their job is to take scriptures, passages, doctrines, and so on and make them accessible and understandable for people. This often means interpreting the information and then finding ways people can apply it to their everyday lives. As a spiritual leader, you will be a scholar for life!

Things to Consider before Becoming a Spiritual Leader

Becoming a spiritual leader is a big responsibility. You are a guide for people's spiritual journeys, so make sure you are up to the task. The way you act will be judged twenty-four hours a day. Your personal and professional lives will be watched very closely. For example, it would look pretty bad if a pastor of a church was screaming at a coach during her son's Little League baseball game. At the same time, a spiritual leader is not supposed to judge others. People come to their spiritual leaders for guidance all the time, and it's the leaders' job to listen and provide acceptance.

A spiritual leader will never be the "ultimate" leader. You are a follower first, of your beliefs. Your goal is to help people strengthen their spirituality through teachings. You will always be surrounded by people who have objections. They may be people with different spiritual beliefs or people who object to just certain areas of your teachings. You will be questioned, doubted, and asked to provide proof. This is one reason you have to be very strong in your beliefs. If you don't believe, then no one else will, and you won't be able to lead.

Most spiritual leaders engage in public speaking at least once a week. It's a major part of the job, and their leadership position depends on them being able to engage and inspire their organizations' members. Speaking in front of people is something that gets easier the more times you do it, so practice whenever you can. You can join your school debate team, participate in drama club, or run a youth group at your place of worship. If you're speaking to employees, volunteers, potential investors, or people looking to you for inspiration, the preparation is the same. It's a lot of work, but it can be very thrilling to have a crowd of people hanging on your every word.

⊛⊛⊛⊛⊛⊛⊛⊛⊛⊛⊛⊛⊛⊛⊛⊛⊛

Name: Adam Hamilton
Job: Pastor of the Church of the Resurrection

Reverend Adam Hamilton founded the United Methodist Church of the Resurrection in Kansas in 1990 with only ninety members. His church now has over eighteen thousand members and is still growing. *Religion and Ethics NewsWeekly* named him one of the "Ten People to Watch in America's Spiritual Landscape." He's won numerous awards, written fourteen books, and in 2013, preached at President Barack Obama's Inaugural Prayer Service. With a large focus on giving back to the community, Pastor Hamilton's church does more than touch people spiritually.

How did you know you wanted to become a spiritual leader?
When I was sixteen years old, several people in my church suggested I had the gifts to be a pastor, and they felt strongly I was

being called by God to do so. My pastor said the same. I did not feel this. But then one week my pastor asked if I would preach for him at the weekend service. It was "youth Sunday." I preached, and though the sermon was horrible, I felt at that moment that this was what God was calling me to do.

In your opinion, what makes a strong leader?
Qualities: integrity, authenticity, passion, great people skills, perseverance, and the ability to make good decisions, to cast a vision for others and to inspire others to pursue the vision.

What leadership skills are important when building a congregation?
I think the same as above—but add to them the ability to effectively preach, a genuine love of people, and a passionate personal conviction of the importance and truth of the Christian gospel.

How did you get comfortable speaking in front of so many people?
The first time I preached, my sermon was horrible. I was nervous, had not adequately prepared, and really did a terrible job. When we started Church of the Resurrection in 1990, I'd had some experience preaching as an associate pastor in a church of several hundred people. Church of the Resurrection started with about ninety people, so I got used to preaching to ninety; then as the church grew, I grew into being comfortable preaching in front of larger congregations. I still feel a bit nervous before getting up to preach each weekend.

What advice would you give students who are looking for leadership experience?
My first leadership experience was working at Hardee's at 105th and Metcalf in Overland Park, Kansas. I learned how to give leadership to the team I worked with. I wasn't technically the leader. My point is that almost every setting or job

has some opportunity to exercise leadership. For years I read everything I could get my hands on on leadership: *Harvard Business Review*, books on leadership from the corporate world, and some church leadership books. When I began trying my hand at leadership in the church, I started small, serving small youth groups, and then grew from there. I also was constantly studying other leaders and seeing what they did well—I still do this.

What current or past leaders have inspired you?
Among Christians, I start with Jesus himself, and the apostles—they are a great study in leadership. I also think of people like John Wesley, the eighteenth-century founder of Methodism. But I also learn leadership from various businesspeople and others. Dr. Martin Luther King Jr. is among my heroes and an excellent study in exercising leadership.

✪✪✪✪✪✪✪✪✪✪✪✪✪✪✪✪✪✪✪✪✪✪

It Takes More Than a Leap of Faith

Becoming a nun or monk in any religion is a serious commitment. The search for a higher purpose requires sacrifice, dedication, and a whole lot of thought and preparation. A person must be prepared to live away from friends and family and give up most worldly possessions. A lot of time will be spent in prayer and quiet time, so the lack of noise can be quite an adjustment.

Many people prepare for this new way of life by making several visits to the monastery or convent where they will be living. If the visits go well, then they may move in as house members. After several years, if everyone decides this is a good fit, then they are allowed to take their vows to officially become monks or nuns. For those people who feel they have a "higher calling," this spiritual journey is worth any sacrifice.

Famous Contemporary Religious Leaders

Billy Graham: This Southern Baptist minister served as a spiritual advisor to many United States presidents and often preached with Martin Luther King Jr. He has preached live to over 200 million people in 185 countries, which is more than any other religious leader in history. He's written thirty-two books and has appeared in the top ten on Gallop's "Most Admired Man" poll a record fifty-seven times.

Tenzin Gyatso: The fourteenth Dalai Lama, which is the head monk of Tibetan Buddhism, is a firm believer in religious harmony—he has spent his life fighting for the welfare of the people of Tibet. In 1989, he received the Nobel Peace Prize for his efforts looking for a peaceful solution between Tibet and the People's Republic of China.

Pope Francis: The current head of the Catholic Church is known for his concern for all of humanity. Inspiring in his down-to-earth approach, he is particularly concerned with poverty. He believes in helping all people regardless of their beliefs or backgrounds. *Fortune* magazine ranked him number one on its "50 Greatest Leaders" list in 2014.

Bartholomew I: The ecumenical patriarch is the archbishop of Constantinople–New Rome for Orthodox Christians but works to promote religious freedom for all people. He has worked with the Roman Catholic Church, various other Christian branches, and Judaism and Islam to strengthen the relationship across various sects. Known as the Green Pope, he works for various environmental causes. *Time* magazine placed him on its "100 Most Influential People in the World" list in 2008.

Rabbi Sharon Kleinbaum: This rabbi of Congregation Beit Simchat Torah (CBST) has a synagogue that welcomes people of all sexual orientations and is an advocate for the LGBT community. She celebrates diversity and speaks out against social injustices. She received the Jewish Funds for Justice Woman of Valor Award and various other prestigious awards. The fight for equality has been documented in many articles she has written in addition to being featured in four films. *Newsweek* placed her on its "50 Most Influential Rabbis in America" list in 2010.

Louis Farrakhan Muhammad: This Nation of Islam leader is known for being outspoken in his social and political views. His Million Man March in Washington, DC, called for all black men to show their commitment to their communities and families by attending his event and listening to speakers such as Maya Angelou, Jesse Jackson, and Martin Luther King Jr.

Sharon Salzberg: Cofounder of the Insight Meditation Society (IMS) and the Barre Center for Buddhist Studies (BCBS), which is one of the most respected meditation centers in the United States, she is a popular public speaker and bestselling author. Magazines and online outlets such as the *Huffington Post, O: The Oprah Winfrey Magazine, Self,* and *Time* magazine have featured her advice and insight into spirituality. The New York Open Center awarded her the honor of Outstanding Contribution to the Mindfulness of the West.

Queen Elizabeth Alexandra Mary: Queen Elizabeth II, constitutional monarch of Commonwealth of Nations, has ruling duties that include being in charge of the Anglican Church of England. She is the church's supreme governor and Defender of the Faith, which are titles she inherited with her crown. She believes religion should play a role in state politics because it provides guidance on how people live their lives and serve their nation. She has been on the

throne for over sixty years and continues to attend many events and to support over six hundred charities.

What to Do When It's Time to Speak Up

Prepare your speech. It's important to know exactly what you want to talk about and the message you want your audience to walk away remembering. This requires organizing your notes. Consider adding personal touches to your speeches through anecdotes or humor to help entertain your audience. This is your time to shine, so do your research and give your audience something they can't get anywhere else.

Make note cards of your key points. You can't deliver your speech by reading it from a piece of paper. This would get a big yawn from your audience. But you can make sure you cover everything in your speech by outlining the main ideas on note cards and having them with you when you speak to your audience.

Practice your speech. Grab a friend or relative and ask that person to listen and make comments. Record yourself, and then you can critique yourself. The more times you practice, the more you'll become comfortable with the material.

Jesse Jackson: This Baptist minister and civil rights activist publicly supports current events involving the black community. Alongside Martin Luther King Jr. and through the organization Southern Christian Leadership Conference (SCLC), he fought for equality among all races. After King's assassination, Jackson decided to run for president of the United States, where he felt he could make more substantial changes involving racial equality, gay rights, and social welfare. After two failed presidential campaigns, he continued to use his influence by negotiating the release of hostages on foreign land. He has received numerous awards, including being named by the 2006 AP-AOL Black Voices poll as the Most Important Black Leader.

David Baruch Lau: At age forty-seven, the chief rabbi of Israel is the youngest ever to be elected to this role. He has modernized his position by teaching *responsa* (Jewish literature) over the internet. In addition to daily radio broadcasts, he appears weekly on a television show for an "Ask a Rabbi" segment. He is the writer and editor of several books and articles.

Sri Mata Amritanandamayi: This Hindu leader is regarded as Amma, the Mother of All, and a spiritual humanitarian. Her followers believe she is a saint and will bring good fortune and well-being to those she physically embraces. She has hugged over 30 million people in the last thirty years. She has published a handful of books and recorded over one thousand devotional songs. In 2014, the *Huffington Post* named her as one of its 50 Powerful Women Religious Leaders.

> A genuine leader is not a searcher for consensus
> but a molder of consensus.[1]
> —MARTIN LUTHER KING JR., PASTOR AND LEADER OF THE
> CIVIL RIGHTS MOVEMENT

✪✪✪✪✪✪✪✪✪✪✪✪✪✪✪✪✪

**Name: Micol Zimmerman Burkeman
Job: Director of the North American
Federation of Temple Youth (NFTY)**

NFTY offers spiritual and personal leadership opportunities to over six thousand high

school students. This is accomplished through local youth groups, regional meetings, and summer camps both locally and abroad. At NFTY Convention, teens are encouraged to participate in a competition to support that year's theme. The theme in 2015 was Myself, My Community, My World and regarded how people interact with and impact their communities. Youth can express this through music, art, videos, and public speaking. NFTY allows teens to get involved at many different levels, including the elected board, which consists of five youths elected by their peers.

Tell us a little about NFTY.

NFTY is the Reform Jewish youth movement in North America, part of the family of Union for Reform Judaism youth camps and programs. For the last seventy-five years, NFTY has offered hundreds of thousands of young people authentic opportunities for teen leadership, enabling our youth to create, lead, and participate in meaningful experiences around social justice, worship, identity and community building, Israel advocacy and engagement, and in truly living meaningful, committed, full Jewish lives. NFTY teens have gone on to form the foundation of our movement's leadership and have helped make this movement what it is today: a beacon of progressive Judaism, committed to egalitarianism, social justice, meaningful Jewish engagement, and supportive and inclusive spiritual communities. NFTY provides a safe and nurturing home for generations of teens to be the people they are and to grow into the people they were meant to be.

What is a principle-centered leader?

A principle-centered leader is someone who practices what they preach. It is easy to stand in front of a community and tell them how they should act in the world—but a principle-centered leader acts in the world as an example to their community. Alignment among what one thinks, says, and does is the sign of a strong leader. Jewish scholar Rabbi Martin Buber once said, "There are three principles in a man's being and life: the principle of thought, the principle of speech, and the principle of action. The origin of all conflict between me and my fellow men is that I do not say what I mean and I don't do what I say." Good leaders say what they mean and do what they say—maybe not all the time, because we're human, after all, but they will always strive to be the examples they wish to set in the world and encourage the same of those around them.

What are the characteristics of a strong spiritual leader? Does this differ from other types of leaders?

Most people go to their leaders seeking answers. What sets spiritual leaders apart from others is their focus on the questions. For a spiritual leader, more important than having and giving answers is helping someone ask the right questions and guiding them as they find meaning for themselves. One of the most pivotal moments in my life happened as a teen. I marched into my father's office and defiantly declared that I no longer believed in God. This might be a shocking moment for any parent, but as the daughter of a rabbi, I had expressed an act of real rebellion, as much against my father as it was against my religion. I stormed in expecting shock and outrage and instead was met with understanding and acceptance. "Our tradition encourages questions," my father gently said. "You should always question—and I'm here to help you explore those questions." That was a turning point for me. And sure enough, learning how to ask thoughtful questions allowed my relationship with Judaism and my relationship with God to grow and develop in a way that no answer that day, or any other day, could have done. Knowing the answers isn't what makes a strong spiritual leader—it's knowing how to help someone ask the right questions and gently guiding that person on the quest for meaning.

What advice would you give teens who are looking for leadership experience?

I would advise teens to look first for meaningful experience. Our strongest leaders didn't necessarily pursue leadership—they aspired to change or improve the world in some way, and by doing something they believed in and that fed their passion, they found the opportunity to lead. I encourage teens to find something they are passionate about, that aligns with their values, and that will benefit more than just themselves. I once heard someone say that the secret to life was finding something that made you truly happy, and doing it for the rest of your life. This can apply to leadership but with a minor tweak: the secret to authentic leadership is finding something that makes you and others around you happy, fulfilled, and better in some way, and doing it for the rest of your life. Leadership opportunities will always present themselves—finding the right place to take the lead is the challenge, and that involves being true to oneself and also thinking beyond oneself. Leading is not about the leader, because you cannot lead others without others. Find the intersection among your passion, your values, and your community —there you will find your opportunity for leadership.

What leaders do you admire?

I admire leaders who care first for their people. Leaders who show deep care and empathy for the community they lead. My father, a rabbi and spiritual leader for over forty years, is one of those leaders and one I always strive to emulate. Congregants may not always remember what he said, but almost all of them continue to talk about the way he made them feel: cared for, nurtured, and significant. From him, I learned that people don't care how much you know until they know how much you care. Good leaders care not just for a cause but also first and foremost for the people they lead.

I also have a deep admiration for the leaders in our NFTY community. Our teens are the heart and soul of our organization. They dedicate their precious and limited time creating and leading meaningful and inspiring experiences for their peers and mobilizing them to make a difference in the world. As I sat with a group of teen leaders this past summer, we started talking about legacy and, specifically, what their legacies would be. After a lively conversation about how they would be remembered, one young woman spoke up and proposed that perhaps the best legacies they could leave shouldn't be about them at all. Their legacies, she continued, should be setting up next year's leaders for success, allowing that group to be remembered even if they never were. True leadership is working to make a difference in the world even when you know you won't directly benefit. Our teens demonstrate that great leaders are not just concerned with their communities' present but also, and perhaps more important, with their communities' future.

✪✪✪✪✪✪✪✪✪✪✪✪✪✪✪✪✪✪✪✪✪✪✪

Characteristics of a Strong Spiritual Leader

★ **Relationships:** they help guide people toward their own spiritual actions and connections.

★ **Self-discovery:** a spiritual leader wants others to reach their full potential and find their purpose.

★ **Transformation:** they build passion in others and encourage them to act on it.

★ **Impact:** their message fills people with hope, peace, and comfort.

★ **Change:** they promote changes in the way people view things, whether it's their past, present, or future.

★ **Serve:** they realize they are serving something larger than themselves.

Have you ever been to a really bad play or other performance? I bet you couldn't wait for it to be over! Now imagine you had to do this week after week. Sounds pretty awful, right? This is why you want to make sure you keep people's attention whenever you are leading a group. Whether you are standing in front of a large group or just a few people, you can practice different ways to keep things interesting. Most spiritual leaders want people to participate during the service. This can be as simple as nodding their heads, swaying to music, or mouthing the words to a prayer. The more they participate, the more actively engaged they are with what you are saying. You can practice this when speaking in front of your class or conducting a club meeting. Try to read your audience by their facial expressions and body language. Do people smile when you make a joke,  or do they roll their eyes? Do people take notes and hang on to your every word, or are they staring out the window? These cues will give you a good idea as to what works and what doesn't work when you are speaking in front of people.

Do people tell you how wonderful the top of your head is? They don't? Then stop bending over and staring at your papers or cue cards! No one wants to look at the top of your head or your back or strain to hear you mumbling. You've done your research and prepared your speech, so look up and be proud of what you are saying. Look people in the eyes and make them feel like you are talking to them. This is the easiest thing to practice because you don't need an audience. Keep eye contact with your friends when you chat during lunch, hold conversations with people without staring down at your cell phone, and use your eyes to let people know you are really listening to them.

Model the way you want other people to act. Have you ever sat through a service or performance where the leader asked you to sing or clap along, but the leader didn't? I know it sounds funny, but it happens more times than you think. Having a great stage presence is all about connecting with people. There's no better way to form a connection with someone than by doing something together. It's like when a song comes on the radio, and you start humming along and then look over and see the person next to you tapping his or her foot. The two of you are having a connection at that moment. You can practice modeling behavior wherever you go. Start clapping during a ball game and watch how other people start joining in, or hold a door open for someone and that person will probably hold another open for someone else. Wear a ribbon to school every Friday to signify some social cause you believe in, and soon people will be asking how they can participate.

✪✪✪✪✪✪✪✪✪✪✪✪✪✪✪✪✪

Name: Cassandra Sanborn
Age: 23
Job (when not studying!): Music minister at Sacred Heart Cathedral

Cassandra Sanborn grew up in the church. Her involvement in youth ministry helped her develop as a person and gain confidence as she moved into a leadership position. Now that she is a college student, she wants to pass that experience to the youth taking her place. In addition to being a music minister, she is a student at the University of Alaska Fairbanks, studying biological sciences with a minor in art. No matter what she does, she wants to put her leadership skills to good use by helping other people.

How did you get involved as a music minister?

In answering how I got involved as a music minister at Sacred Heart Cathedral, I would say that when there is a need, it gets filled! The music leader who had been covering the liturgical music was leaving on and off during the summer (and permanently at the end of the summer—she became a nun!). At this time, I was not taking any courses, so I hesitantly agreed to cover these masses. At the time, I only knew a few chords on my guitar, and I had never led in music before. I was nervous, and it was shaky at first! But with the help and support of the singers, it came to be something I grew more confident in and really enjoyed. I then realized that I was reaching out to people and youth through music and helping them connect at church. I continue to do music even today. These feelings translated straight into leading youth ministry as well.

What leadership skills do you use?

Leadership skills include confidence, humility, punctuality, respect, attention, forgiveness, preparedness, positive attitude, flexibility, knowledge in the field, love of learning, and attention.

What is the difference between a spiritual leader and other types of leaders?

The difference [is that] being a spiritual leader versus any other type of leader requires you to open yourself to others in a pretty intense way. When it comes to spirituality, it is centered on you and your experiences on a completely new level, if you are open to it. It is about forming a community not only with other people but also with God. It is a three-way dynamic, and it is powerful and can change lives. Leading something like this is huge. When it comes to spirituality, no one is on the same page in their journey, including yourself. Being a spiritual leader may seem hard, but if you do your best, it becomes easy.

What advice would you give teens who are interested in becoming spiritual leaders?
My advice to any youth who want to become a spiritual leader or to those who never have considered it is to try. Do your best and follow your passion. Be confident in yourself, because you can achieve more than you ever thought you could. Respect those in authority, and you will receive it by your peers. Accept people around you where they are at. Don't be afraid of mistakes, because you are always learning, even when you are the ripe old age of twenty-three!

What have you learned from leading other people?
I have learned more about my faith and my limitations. Most importantly, I have learned more about myself and my talents. It is amazing how much you can learn while leading! I am now finishing my last year of college and look forward to continuing with leading at my church and wherever God takes me!

✪✪✪✪✪✪✪✪✪✪✪✪✪✪✪✪✪✪✪✪✪✪✪✪

8

Get Environmental

Look outside your window and hopefully you see trees, maybe some birds, and a clear sky. All of this is important to environmentally conscious leaders, because their mission is to preserve our natural environment. Environmental conservation is the act of protecting the habitats of animals and plants. This includes problems we've created over the years like contamination, forest destruction, and pollution. Environmental protection is often conducted on a national basis through the government and nonprofit agencies. You can do your part on an individual basis just by recycling your trash. This prevents overcrowding our landfills and allows your trash to be reused.

There are many leadership opportunities available in environmental conservation. Education is necessary for a great environmental impact to be made, so people are aware of the problems and willing to make the necessary changes to provide a solution. Many great environmental organizations would love to have people to spread their messages and inform the public about how they can help.

An important component of protecting the Earth is getting laws passed. For example, endangered species' protection allows animals to reproduce and hopefully avoid extinction. Many laws exist on how companies are allowed to get rid of their waste, so they minimize the damage they do to land or water. You don't have to be a politician or an environmental lawyer to get a law passed. All you need are some leadership skills and passion for your project to get started!

How's Your Environment?

Are you curious about the quality of the air, water, and land where you live? If so, visit the government's Environmental Protection Agency site at epa.gov/myenvironment. You can search by city, zip code, or even your home address. There is a feature that allows you to create and print maps based on your search. This is a great opportunity for you to take charge and take steps to improve where you live. You can use this information to make changes in your household to make it more environmentally friendly.

✪✪✪✪✪✪✪✪✪✪✪✪✪✪✪

Name: Laura Segura
Job: Founder of the National Teen Leadership Program

Laura Segura retired in 2015 from the nonprofit she founded in 1992. The first year of the National Teen Leadership Program (NTLP), 185 teens attended her leadership camp. Now, over twenty years later, she has worked with over twelve thousand teens. NTLP offers camp, a diversity day, and Change the World awards. In 2002, Segura was rewarded for her work by being asked to be an Olympic torchbearer. In 2006 and 2009, NTLP was awarded the Excellence in Education Award. Although Segura will surely be missed, her legacy will continue to grow.

Describe NTLP.

For twenty-two years, the award-winning National Teen Leadership Program (NTLP) has provided leadership camps that motivate and inspire the leader within every teen. Overnight camps are held on college campuses and include motivational speakers, leadership exercises, small group sessions, interactive workshops, interviews with business professionals, and a recognition ceremony. We are a certified Presidential Volunteer Service Award organization and award students for their outstanding achievements in volunteer service, academics, extracurricular activities, and athletics. We're fun too! The program also includes a dance, hypnotist show, and connections with great teens from all over the US. It's open to teens from all over the US in eighth through twelfth grades.

It's hard to describe NTLP as a leadership camp, although what we do becomes leadership down [the] road. We are more about motivating young people to think outside the box and outside themselves. To understand that it is within their power to make a difference and that they *must* be the person to make that difference, as if no one else will. We try to instill self-confidence when most teens feel insecure and to provide a safe haven where they can express their thoughts and feelings and know that others often feel the same. We do this by providing team-building and team-bonding exercises and small group sessions that produce aha moments. We engage speakers that can reach inside and make them feel powerful about their abilities. All these concepts and strategies make better individuals who hopefully leave our program feeling lifted up, confident, and secure about who they are, and, ultimately, who are better leaders.

How did it get started?

I was a meeting planner by trade, working for American Express Travel. A work acquaintance I met introduced me to his program that he was running in Minnesota and Wisconsin, which involved leadership weekends for teens. He asked me if I would set one up for him in California, which I did in 1992. I took over the program in 1993.

Why is it important for teens to gain leadership skills?

Our youth are our future. More than just leadership skills, they need a huge dose of self-confidence, the ability to stand up to peer pressure, to know the difference between leading and following, to know they can set the bar high and achieve anything they set their sights on, that taking personal respon-sibility and becoming open-minded about others' differences are paramount, that winning is not as important as having a winning team, and that giving back to someone is giving back to everyone. If they can achieve these values while they are young, they will hopefully be on the right track to becoming successful, open-minded, motivated, caring, ethical, respon-sible adults.

Can you give me a couple of examples of how your alumni have applied the leadership skills they've learned at your camp?

Right away, the ones who come to my mind are the young men and women who serve on our board of directors. They took the skills they learned at camp and returned to staff the programs after they graduated high school. Our board chair, vice chair, and treasurer are all NTLP alumni who attended from 1993 to 1996. After all these years, they are still giving back to a program they maintain motivated them to make positive differences in the world. They recognize that by returning and helping to motivate the current generation of teens, they are propagating a world full of teens who will also grow up to care and want to give back. Thus, the ripple effect.

What advice would you give teens who would like to gain leadership skills now?

Take advantage of NTLP and of every other leadership program available, get involved in clubs at school, spend some time in your community giving back in some way, don't judge others until you've walked in their shoes, sit with a different clique at lunch, invite people to your clique, don't believe everything you see and hear in media and social media. Do the research and find out the truth. Know that someone is always watching you—a younger sibling, friend, teacher, parent. Are you someone they can be proud of or someone they are ashamed of? Speak up when you see someone being hurt and tell someone when you feel hurt yourself.

What leaders do you admire?

My parents, who raised me to be tolerant, open-minded, caring, thoughtful. For sixty-eight years of marriage (to date), they have been the perfect role models who embody the golden rule, care more about others than they do themselves, value ethics and honesty above all else, and have taught love and respect through their own examples. At ninety-six and ninety-two, they still volunteer, attend their neighborhood watch meetings, man the polling booths during elections, and stay up-to-date on current events. Other than that, I admire leaders who do the right thing because it's the right thing to do and not for political gain.

✪✪✪✪✪✪✪✪✪✪✪✪✪✪✪✪✪✪✪✪✪✪

Never doubt that a small group of thoughtful,
committed citizens can change the world;
indeed, it's the only thing that ever has.[1]
—MARGARET MEAD, ANTHROPOLOGIST

Bindi Irwin

Not many people would see a connection between being an award-winning conservationist and a first-place winner in a dance contest, but Bindi Irwin proved that she could do it. She's been in the spotlight since age two, when she began appearing next to her dad on television in the *The Crocodile Hunter*. His show became hugely popular due to his outgoing personality, and the entire family became well-known due to the show. He died in 2006 after a stingray strike and Bindi decided to continue his conservation work. At the age of nine she recorded a twenty-six-episode wildlife show for the Discovery Channel, and an environmental hero was born.

The world has literally watched Bindi grow up as she continues to spread her messages about environmental conservation. She was born and still lives on the Sunshine Coast in Queensland, Australia; she works there at the Australia Zoo. Her goal is to make a difference by promoting wildlife protection, empowering other people to get involved, and educating people about animals. She raises awareness by appearing on television programs, writing news pieces, and making public appearances.

In addition to working at the zoo, she has become involved in several other causes. In 2013 she became a youth ambassador for Sustainable Population Australia to preserve animal habitats. In 2014 she became a Brisbane Lions ambassador. She also creates videos and blogs for SeaWorld as an envoy to promote conservation to kids. As if that doesn't keep her busy enough, she partnered with Unitywater to ask people to stop using disposable water bottles and to drink tap water to prevent plastic from getting into rivers and oceans. These are some of the many reasons she was awarded the Australian Young Conservationist Award in 2014. With all of her achievements due to hard work, no one was surprised when she also became the 2015 winner of the show *Dancing With the Stars*. Her star quality shines through whether she's on or off the stage!

Fourteen of the
Top Environmental Organizations

Center for a New American Dream hopes to help Americans reduce consumption, which will help protect the environment and encourage communities to work together. If you would like to organize projects for your community, then visit newdream.org and download the Community Action Kit.

Greenpeace International is an organization that exposes environmental problems, and asks people to find a solution. Previous victories include: fashion retailer Zara pledged to eliminate the use of hazardous chemicals in production, and Lego ended its promotion contract with Shell in protest of its plans to drill for oil in the Arctic. You can participate now at greenpeace.org by joining a campaign or volunteering at a local Greenpeace office.

Earth Policy Institute (EPI) works with the media, lawmakers, professors, environmentalists, and businesses to lead the world along a more environmentally friendly and sustainable path. The organization hopes to accomplish this by ending poverty, rebuilding ecosystems, and stabilizing the climate and the earth's population. The website, earth-policy.org, provides you with all the information you need to take action and lead your community toward a more sustainable future.

Environmental Defense Fund (EDF) works with businesses, farmers, and scientists to find solutions to issues concerning the oceans, ecosystems, health, climate, and energy. Internships, listed at edf.org, will take you from Capitol Hill to the wetlands.

Friends of the Earth provides environmental and social services in over seventy-four countries. Members campaign on issues such as climate change, human rights, small-scale farming, and keeping forests intact. If you want to help out, you can go to foei.org for volunteer opportunities.

Humane Society is the largest animal protection agency. The organization rescues animals and finds them homes and pushes for stronger laws to protect animals' rights. To find out about the many local and national volunteer opportunities, connect with the volunteer center at humanesociety.org. Also, you can access a document called "55 Ways to Help Animals" that has wonderful suggestions for leadership opportunities you can take at your school or in the community.

National Audubon Society protects animal habitats, with a concentration on birds. There are over five hundred chapter offices. You can take action by signing up for a campaign and emailing government representatives on different issues affecting wildlife at audubon.org.

National Geographic Society is one of the largest nonprofit scientific organizations in the world that focuses on the planet. Donations support education, exploration, conservation, different cultures, and research. You can get involved by applying for a grant for exploration projects, applying for a society membership, or completing some of their educational activities at education.nationalgeographic.com.

National Resources Defense Council (NRDC) is one of America's most influential environmental groups, with over 1.4 million members, activists, and lawyers. Current focus is on global warming, endangered species, pollution, clean water, and the ocean's ecosystems. Visit nrdc.org to join an action campaign or to view internship opportunities. You will gain environmental law exposure along with the opportunity to lead our planet toward a brighter future.

Project ORANGS

In 2007, Rhiannon Tomtishen and Madison Vorva started Project ORANGS (Orangutans Really Appreciate and Need Girl Scouts) in order to earn a Girl Scout Bronze Award. Their mission was to raise awareness about how the endangered orangutans were losing their habitats to people planting palm oil plantations. Little did they know, but palm oil was an ingredient in Girl Scout cookies! They began an online campaign resulting in over seventy thousand emails being sent to the CEO of the Girl Scouts asking to make their cookies safe for rainforests. The campaign worked, and the Girl Scouts' organization is now committed to making their cookies rainforest friendly.

National Wildlife Federation is dedicated to protecting animals and their homes. This organization coordinates activities with other nonprofit conservation organizations in forty-nine states. Check out the extensive volunteer network at nwf.org.

Ocean Conservancy works to keep the ocean healthy, in clean water, clean beaches, healthy fish, and thriving marine life. You can sign up for the email list at oceanconservancy.org.

Sierra Club has been around since 1892 and is the largest environmental group, with over 2 million supporters. Their mission is to protect the wilderness and endangered species, along with ensuring we have clean air and water. The strong teen program, through the Sierra Student Coalition (SSC), has more than thirteen thousand active students. If you'd like to lead the way to a better environment, then check out sierraclub.org.

Surfrider is focused on protecting the ocean and beaches. Core efforts are clean water, beach access, and beach preservation. There is an entire website devoted to youth involvement. Leadership opportunities include starting a Quad club at your school, volunteering at a local office, or starting a service project. For everything you need to get started, visit surfrider.org/quad.

World Wildlife Fund (WWF) works to conserve nature and to protect endangered animals and their habitats. WWF operates in one hundred countries and has 5 million members globally. It offers a diverse range of career opportunities as well as college internships and grants, which can be found at worldwildlife.org.

✪✪✪✪✪✪✪✪✪✪✪✪✪✪✪✪✪

Name: Jonny Cohen
Age: 19
Job (when not studying!): Founder of GreenShield

Jonny Cohen is passionate about encouraging youth to pursue their dreams. When he was in seventh grade, he had a big idea to make school buses more efficient. He founded GreenShields to develop an aerodynamic device that increases gas mileage by redirecting airflow and decreasing drag. The device costs approximately $500, but a bus can recoup that cost within a year because of money saved on gas.

He's received several grants and awards and has been featured in *Scientific American* and the *Huffington Post* and on *Good Morning America*. Jonny is a nineteen-year-old sophomore at Columbia University studying mechanical engineering. You can read more about his amazing school buses at his group's website, greenshieldsproject.com.

Describe your company, GreenShields.
GreenShields designs, tests, and builds aerodynamic add-on devices that attach to the tops of school buses, increasing gas mileage approximately 10 percent, decreasing CO_2 emissions, and saving gas and money for schools.

How did it get started?
When I was walking home from school one day in seventh grade, I thought of the idea. I was taking an enrichment Saturday class about aerodynamics at Northwestern University, and I noticed the box-shaped school buses parked in front of my junior high, and I thought that a school bus could be made more aerodynamic. The inefficient design of the school buses bothered me; I wanted to do something about it—so I ran home and told my older sister Azza about my idea. She took me to visit her freshman physics teacher, Mr. Pujara, and he told me he thought my idea could work. Here is a link to a brief video that describes the beginning of GreenShields. *GreenShields: School Buses to Save the Planet!* youtube.com/watch?v=BV85JRujpks.

How do you manage college and running your own company at the same time?
It is definitely a challenge to work on GreenShields and be a student at the same time, but I have found my professors at Columbia to be very supportive. For example, I missed a week of school this year to attend meetings at the White House and State Department, since I am a youth advisor to the USA Science and Engineering Festival. Also, during my freshman year, I missed a week of school to teach a class

on green product design for high school students at NuVu Studios in Cambridge. I really enjoy my classes at Columbia; however, when opportunities arise to hopefully inspire kids or advance GreenShields, I just go and worry about catching up on my work later! I'm also involved in a green technology start-up, Ecoviate, with Param Jaggi. I met Param in 2012 at the Forbes 30 under 30 event in New York. I was named to the energy list in 2012 and 2013. Finally, I work as a product design consultant at Medline Industries. The entrepreneurial environment at Columbia encourages engagement with New York City and globally, so I'm lucky to be at a school that supports aspiring innovators.

What do you think makes a strong leader?
Knowing when to ask for help and finding experts smarter than you that you can learn from. It's important to collaborate, listen, and learn from your mistakes. It is essential to feel genuine passion and excitement for your venture. Don't be afraid to think out of the box to solve problems. Most importantly, a strong leader must have integrity and be humble—always.

What skills can students start developing now to become leaders in the future?
Anyone, regardless of age, can be a leader and a changemaker in society. Students should take the time to think about a problem facing society that they care about and feel a passion for and then take responsibility by trying to do something—small steps and small actions matter. By beginning to solve a problem and breaking it down into small steps and actions, students are learning responsibility and how to execute. Learning to build a team, delegating, and taking action are skills that everyone needs to build. Start a recycling club at school or in your community, for example. Raise money for a cause you care about by organizing a bake sale. Anything is possible if you try; however, nothing will change if you don't try.

What current or past leaders have inspired you and why?
The leaders who have always inspired me are scientists; to me, they lead society and humanity forward. Albert Einstein, Nikola Tesla, and Leonardo da Vinci are inspiring leaders because even though they are different and addressed different innovation in science, their determination in the face of society's doubts motivates me. They thought without boundaries, and I try to do that as well.

What advice would you give students who are looking to gain leadership experience right now?
Find a mentor—it can be a teacher, a parent, an adult—who can give you guidance and is someone you can brainstorm with to help you find your passion. Then just go for it—ask some friends to help you and seek out help from a local Rotary Club, Boy and Girl Scouts organizations, or your local high school, even if you are not in high school yet. Attend leadership conferences through the Points of Light Foundation, Youth Service America, and Ashoka's Youth Venture. Join clubs at your school and in your community that you are interested in and don't worry about your age—you are never too young to try to change the world!

What challenges have you faced in setting up your first company?
Overcoming regulations so schools can use the GreenShield has been my biggest challenge.

✪✪✪✪✪✪✪✪✪✪✪✪✪✪✪✪✪✪✪✪✪✪✪✪

Challenge
Be a Young Scientist

Do you have what it takes to solve an everyday problem by using science, math, and technology in your solution?

This problem may directly affect you or be something that affects your community or is a global issue. The Discovery Education 3M Young Scientist Challenge gives youth in grades five through eight the opportunity to submit a video of their discovery. Judges pick ten finalists who get to participate in a summer mentor program before competing in the main event, where a grand prize of $25,000 and a trip to an exotic location (like Costa Rica) are awarded. It may sound difficult, but let's see if you're up to the challenge.

The first step to getting started is to visit the contest website at youngscientistchallenge.com. Here you will find all of the details you need to enter the contest, along with videos and advice from prior participants. Winners in the past have invented everything from a way to eliminate texting while driving, to turning grass waste into electricity, to creating sandbags that reduce flood damage caused by salt water. As you can see, the only limit to project ideas is your imagination!

What if you have a great idea but aren't sure how to execute it? No problem! That's where the mentorship program kicks in. The lucky ten finalists are matched up with a scientist from the 3M Corporation. The scientist will help you with brainstorming sessions, advice, and ideas to explore.

Are you wondering how your video will be judged? Do you need to be a movie producer or have access to expensive equipment? Of course not! This is all about your idea and the science behind it. Your idea and solution will be judged on the following criteria:

★ **Creativity (30 percent):** Is this a new idea?

★ **Scientific Knowledge (30 percent):** Do you have research to back this up?

★ **Persuasiveness (20 percent):** Can you communicate your enthusiasm for this project and why it is necessary?

★ **Overall Presentation (20 percent):** Is the information presented in a way that is understandable?

The website provides all of the tools you need to get started. Now it's just up to you to put on your thinking cap and come up with the next great solution to an everyday problem. Being a scientific leader can be a lot of fun, and being a problem solver is a great reward!

9

Get Executive

When you think of a big corporation, what comes to mind? Is it online companies like eBay and Google? Maybe it makes you think of products you use every day like Coke or Nike? Or where your parents go to shop like Walmart and Barnes and Noble? Regardless of the business, they all have one thing in common—they all needed strong leadership to become the corporate giants they are today.

> **No man will make a great leader who wants to do it all himself, or to get all the credit for doing it.**[1]
>
> —ANDREW CARNEGIE, PHILANTHROPIST
> AND SELF-MADE TYCOON

Name: Brooke Martin
Age: 14
Job (when not studying!): Founder of iCPooch

Brooke Martin is the innovator, inventor, and founder of iCPooch, which is a product that allows you to video-chat with your dog when you are away from the house. Not only can you talk to your furry friend but you can remotely give him or her a treat. She was awarded first runner-up in the Discovery Education 3M Young Scientist Challenge in 2013 and has been featured in the *Wall Street Journal* and the *New York Times* and on the *NBC Nightly News* and many other news outlets. In addition to her work with iCPooch, she is active in her community. She has received the Chase Youth Award for Middle School Leadership, the Distinguished Student Award from the Washington Association of Educators of the Talented and Gifted, and is a high school honor student. At age fourteen, she's proof that you're never too young to pursue your passion.

Describe iCPooch and how you came up with the idea.
iCPooch was born as a result of an eighth-grade class project I did on entrepreneurship. I decided as part of my project to participate in an intense fifty-four-hour event called Startup Weekend Spokane, held in September of 2012 at Gonzaga University in Spokane, Washington. I wanted to know firsthand what it meant to be an entrepreneur. First I needed to come up with an idea that I could pitch to a large group of adults.

My dog, Kayla, suffered from anxiety whenever we would leave her at home alone. She was so unhappy when we were gone. My friends and I would often Skype with each other, and I thought it would be great if there was a way to check in on your pup to make sure they were okay. I did some online research and found out that over 10 million dogs suffer from separation anxiety in the US alone. Kayla really likes her cookies, so I thought it would be even better if you could not only video-chat with your pet but also be able to deliver them a tasty treat.

Not knowing how the adults would receive me, on Friday evening I presented my innovative idea in the one-minute pitch time allowed to all participants. I was one of forty presenters (thirty-nine adults and me). I ended up receiving the most votes of any pitch presented. Afterward, I was able to form a team of professionals that helped me to further develop my idea over the weekend. Everyone was so supportive to iCPooch and me.

How did you figure out how to get your product made and how to get your business started?
After Startup Weekend Spokane was over, I talked with my parents, and they were so supportive of my idea. They asked me if I wanted to continue to pursue the idea to see how far it could go. I said yes! At this point, iCPooch was just a concept. Soon after, my dad and I started working on prototypes in our garage. After a couple of months of design experimenting, we were finally ready to go to the next level. I started contacting many of the adult professionals I had met at Startup Weekend Spokane to ask for their support. I had software developers, designers, engineers, marketing specialists, patent attorneys, and others who were anxious to lend me their assistance. I was only twelve years old, but they all wanted to help me succeed.

How does it feel to be a leader and the youngest employee of a company?
I've always enjoyed being involved in leadership. I've been a Girl Scout since age four and have participated in a number of leadership roles throughout my school experience. Being a leader during the development of iCPooch has given me the opportunity to work with many adult professionals who have helped me to develop my leadership skills even further. While

I'm the youngest member of our team, I consistently receive positive support from those around me. No one treats me any different because I'm young; they respect me for how hard I'm working and for what I'm trying to accomplish.

What leadership skills have you learned from starting a business?

I've learned many skills during the process of developing iCPooch. I've learned gratitude, hard work, perseverance, teamwork, positive attitude, and fearlessness.

What challenges have you faced during this process?

About a year into the creation of iCPooch, with many of our initial start-up challenges behind us, we launched our first crowdfunding effort in the form of a Kickstarter campaign. The key to a successful crowdfunding effort is to set your fundraising goals high enough to satisfy your immediate needs for capital but at low enough levels that they are attainable—because it's an all-in or all-out proposition. If you don't raise funds to meet or exceed your stated target, your project sees none of the money. Buoyed by the incredible support around me, I strategically, and somewhat overconfidently, set my goal, and the campaign was off and running. The initial response was amazing. In a matter of hours, we were well on the board with pledges rapidly accumulating—and within days, iCPooch's Kickstarter campaign was being featured in the national press on such amazing venues as *GeekWire*, *Yahoo*, and *NBC Nightly News*. And just as it seemed there would be no stopping us, our Kickstarter campaign completely plateaued!

By the end of the campaign, we'd raised a respectable amount of funding but only 30 percent of our target. And that's where my real education began—at the painful juncture between the highest highs and the lowest lows, where I was forced to dig in, refocus on my dream, and begin again. I realized I still had a viable product, an incredible team of support, and an awesome opportunity to succeed. As I moved into refining the project, and as my determination grew along with my humility, I learned the value of perseverance in entrepreneurship. Six months later, with renewed focus and determination, we launched a new Kickstarter campaign that reached 150 percent of our project goal.

How important is time management and delegation to your role as a company leader?
Time management is very important, especially when you're a full-time high school student. It takes a team of individuals to successfully run a company. I've been so fortunate to have an amazing group of professionals who help me with the day-to-day operations of my business. I can't emphasize enough how important it is to have the right people on your team and to empower them to use their skills. This is why I think the most important leadership attribute is gratitude to those who contribute to our successes along the way.

What advice would you give teens who have an idea for a new product?
Any idea is only as good as your ability to get it to the finish line. Don't be afraid to ask adults for support—they'll be more than willing to help you achieve your goals if you stay focused and committed to your success. Looking back, I can't believe the journey that my life has taken me on the past two years, all because it wasn't enough to just have a good idea. iCPooch is now available for sale and is being shipped worldwide.

✪✪✪✪✪✪✪✪✪✪✪✪✪✪✪✪✪✪✪✪✪✪✪

Where C-level Is Much Better Than Average

Every organization or company has a hierarchy when it comes to its leadership structure. At your school, the order may be principal, vice principal, heads of academic departments, teachers, teacher assistants, and then students. Most companies are led by a team of C-level executives. These "chiefs" set the tone, mission, and goals for the corporation. They are responsible for hiring and delegating tasks to meet those objectives. If you're going to work in the business world, why not aim for the top? Here are a few titles for you to consider:

Chief Executive Officer (CEO)

A CEO or president is the big kahuna of the company. This is the highest-ranking position you can get! In this job, you'll make major decisions and be in charge of the company's growth. The details of your plans will be carried out by managers and executives who work for you. If you want to be a CEO, then you'd better be prepared to work hard, have a head for business, and be good at making decisions.

Chief Operations Officer (COO)

A COO or vice president works hand in hand with the company CEO. This job requires you to make the day-to-day operations run more smoothly and efficiently. You are the eyes and ears of the organization for the CEO and will be required to give reports on how the company is running. If you want this job, then be prepared to understand every department in the company. From knowing about marketing to information technology, you will be expected to be a jack- or jill-of-all-trades.

Chief Financial Officer (CFO)

A CFO supervises the accounting and finance departments of a company. If you have a head for numbers and might like to keep

A Day in the Life of a Business Leader

A business leader often has several different projects going on at once, and lots of people want that person's attention. A strong leader needs to know how to multitask and get things done quickly. Here's an example of how a corporate leader might schedule the day.

6:00 AM Rise and shine.

6:30–8:30 AM Exercise, eat breakfast, and commute to work.

8:30–9:30 AM Read and respond to emails and texts.

9:30–10:00 AM Go over schedule for the day/week.

10:00–11:00 AM Conduct a meeting.

11:00 AM–Noon Work on a project.

Noon–1:00 PM Have a business lunch with another executive.

1:00–2:00 PM Catch up on emails, texts, and phone calls.

2:00–3:00 PM Attend an afternoon meeting or conference call.

3:00–5:00 PM Work with a team on a task or project.

5:00–6:00 PM Finish up paperwork and look over the schedule for the next day.

6:00–10:00 PM Spend time with the family, while occasionally answering a business text or email on the cell phone.

10:00–10:30 PM Engage in personal development by reading a business book or industry news before bed.

10:30 PM Turn out the lights!

a balance sheet, then this is the ultimate job for you. The responsibilities for you and your team will include maintaining a budget, watching the cash flow, and keeping track of contracts. When the CEO has a question about money, you will be the person who is contacted.

Chief Information Officer (CIO)

A CIO manages the technology of a company, from computer hardware to software to training. The size and type of company determines how many technical people may work for a CIO, but in larger companies, it takes a very large staff to keep all of the computer systems running. Most companies have a lot of sensitive information, so computer security is constantly being monitored and updated. If you like to keep up on current technology and come up with solutions for how to make things run more efficiently, then becoming a technology leader may be the job for you.

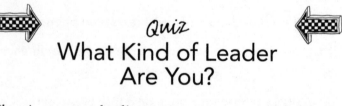

Quiz
What Kind of Leader Are You?

When it comes to leading a sports team or a school project or organizing a fundraiser, it's important to understand what leadership qualities you have and what qualities you may want to work on. A great leader likes to build the team up instead of tearing the team down. Take this short quiz to see what kind of leader you are—you can record your answers on a separate sheet of paper—and learn where you may improve.

In a meeting, you would . . .
    A. Address the group yourself

B. Start the meeting and then let each group leader speak

C. Have somebody else conduct it

Why do people like to have a leader?
A. They don't, but what choice do they have?

B. To have someone create a vision for the group.

C. So they don't have to do it.

Should a leader take the suggestions of other group members?
A. A leader should take charge and make the decisions.

B. Using people's ideas is a great way to use everyone's strengths.

C. Why not? It makes their job easier.

You are falling behind on a deadline, so you . . .
A. Work twenty-four hours a day to get it done

B. Inspire the team to pitch in and get it done

C. Have everyone work late to get everything done

You miss a deadline, so you . . .
A. Take full responsibility

B. As a team, figure out why the deadline didn't work and how to make it next time

C. Shrug it off and move on

What do you do if someone isn't pulling his or her weight?
A. Pull them aside and find out what's going on and share what I expect.

B. Reevaluate that person's strengths and see if he or she can contribute another way.

C. Get rid of that person once and for all.

What's your favorite type of teacher?

A. Someone who's super organized and gives great lectures

B. Someone who has everyone sit in a circle and participate in group discussions

C. A teacher who shows a lot of films and assigns little homework

Your dream is to . . .

A. Work your way up to a leadership position

B. Start a project with your friends

C. Win a bunch of cash

You are speaking in front of a group, and everyone's being loud and obnoxious, so you . . .

A. Tell everyone to pay attention in a forceful voice

B. Ask for everyone's cooperation

C. Cancel the meeting since no one is paying attention

When it comes to clothes, you feel a leader should . . .

A. Dress professionally to set the right tone

B. Wear comfortable and casual clothes, so everyone feels equal

C. Not give it a second thought

If you answered mostly As, then you are an autocratic leader, which means that what you say rules. You like to make all of the decisions without other people's opinions or help. Taking charge lets the rest of the group focus on their tasks. Caution: This type of leader can easily become bossy or controlling.

If you answered mostly Bs, then you are a participatory leader. This type of leadership operates a group like a democracy, where everyone has a right to speak up and give input. Everyone has a role to play when decisions are made, and everything feels like a team effort. Caution: This type of environment takes patience since decisions may need to be discussed with various people before they are made. Also, some people may not want to be part of the decision-making process.

If you answered mostly Cs, then you may be a laissez-faire leader who likes to hand things off to other people. Your followers have the freedom to make all of their own choices. Caution: You are going to have a hard time getting things done if you use this leadership style. Without your guidance, projects, deadlines, and expectations are harder to meet.

✪✪✪✪✪✪✪✪✪✪✪✪✪✪✪

Name: Timothy D. McGuirk
Job: Director of emergency services at James H. Haley Veterans' Hospital

VIP profile

Dr. Timothy McGuirk is a retired captain in the United States Navy, Medical Corps. His career in emergency medicine and as a flight surgeon transferred him to exciting places all over the world, like Spain and Japan.

During his career in the military, he received the Meritorious Service Medal with Gold Star, Navy Commendation Medal, Navy Meritorious Unit Commendation, and Coast Guard Meritorious Unit Commendation, in addition to many other awards and decorations. His role in the navy helped to prepare him for his fast-paced job as the director of emergency services for the Veterans' Hospital in Tampa, Florida.

What is your role as a leader?
As the director of the emergency department, I have to make sure the entire staff works together as a team. I start that process by recognizing and acknowledging that every member of the team is vital, and I encourage and empower every member of the team to participate in developing emergency department processes and systems. Having perspectives from all members of the team can help ensure buy-in for the processes, and it will hopefully make those processes run smoother.

I also see my role as a mentor for the staff. There are many challenging situations in the emergency department, and most have little to do with medicine. Dealing with patients or family members who are angry about having to wait to be seen or about the food or about the dose of morphine that was ordered can be very difficult to deal with. Then there are the consultants who you call at 3:00 AM on a Saturday to take out an appendix. Those consultants are not always happy to receive a call.

There are sometimes internal conflicts between emergency department staff members. I find the best way to handle these situations is to be on the floor helping to monitor the flow and stepping in when necessary. I can't be there 24/7, but by having open discussions with the staff about how to handle particular situations, I have observed improved performance. I won't be there forever, so I have to make sure I train the folks who will take over for me.

I continue to work in the emergency department as a staff physician to keep up my skills, so I can continue to earn the respect of my staff. From time to time I will go in on night shifts or weekend shifts to help fill in if someone is sick. The emergency department runs 24/7, 365 days a year, and I think it's important to work with the staff on all shifts.

What leadership roles exist in the emergency department of a hospital?

Leadership is about taking responsibility for the care of the patients there. Every member of the emergency department team is a leader from time to time. If a nurse goes into a patient's room in response to an alarm and finds the patient is not breathing, the nurse will call a code blue to get the emergency department team to the room, but until the team gets there, that nurse is in charge. That nurse is the situational leader until the physician arrives. Once the physician enters the room, that person will take over the leadership role for the code blue. Let's say one of the intravenous pumps delivering potentially lifesaving medication starts to alarm due to a problem. Very few physicians are trained to troubleshoot pumps, so the nurse will become the situational leader again and take charge of fixing the problem.

What makes working for the emergency department different than other leadership roles?

The emergency department is a very dynamic environment. You never know what will come through your doors next. It could be several patients from a multicar pileup on an icy road, dozens of patients from a mass casualty event, or a patient with a serious disease or infection. Emergency department physicians, nurses, and technicians have to be very creative, and they have to work together in order to get the job done. Emergency department leadership must ensure that the emergency department has the right people with the right skills and training and the right equipment to get the job done right the first time. We don't often get a second chance.

What are the challenges to this job?

Emergency departments throughout the country are over-crowded, understaffed, and underequipped, and they can be very difficult places to work. You might have every bed filled, the waiting room overflowing, and be on diversion so no ambulances are supposed to come, but a car can pull up with a passenger in the front seat who has stopped breathing. You can't say, "Sorry, ma'am, we're full. You'll have to drive to the next hospital down the street." We have to work quickly and think outside the box.

Burnout is a real problem. Part of my role is to monitor and support morale. I try to let the staff know their work is really appreciated, and I make sure my boss and the rest of the hospital leadership knows how much I appreciate their dedication and hard work. In my experience, we often only hear from the boss when there is a perceived screwup. We are all human, and we all make mistakes, so we have to design systems with cross checks and failsafe procedures so our mistakes are caught before they reach the patient.

What should students know about working for a hospital?

While the emergency department is a very stressful place to work, it is also very rewarding. We will take care of anyone, at any time, with any complaint. We treat first and ask questions later. We are available when no one else is. We have access to virtually every service and resource at our hospital 24/7/365. If our hospital doesn't have the required service, we can transfer the patient via ambulance, or even via helicopter if necessary, to get the patient to the facility that has the required service. Despite the long waits, the overcrowding, and the strong personalities often found in the emergency department, I believe all Americans are glad we have an extensive emergency medicine system in this country, and I am proud to be a part of it.

★ ★

Young CEOs on the Rise

Here are some inspiring leaders who are making waves.

Suhas Gopinath: Born in 1986, he founded a multinational technology company called Global INC. at the age of fourteen. For many years he was considered to be the "World's Youngest CEO," and he went on to earn a degree from Harvard University. Over the years he's taken his business out of a home office and into an international success.

Sindhuja Rajaraman: Born in 1997, she founded an animation production company called Seppan at the age of fourteen. This all stemmed from her passion for drawing and cartoons. She is a brand ambassador for Corel Software and hopes to attend film school one day.

Harli Jordean: Born in 2003, he founded Land of Marbles at the age of eight. This started because he loved playing and eventually collecting marbles with his friends. His obsession led him to the internet, where he realized how hard it was to find quality marbles. Deciding he could do better, he launched his own site to sell marbles and became a "Marble King."

Shravan Kumaran and Sanjay Kumaran: Shravan, age fifteen, and Sanjay, age fourteen, are the brothers behind the mobile phone app company called GoDimensions. These programmers have created ten apps ranging from alphabet games, car racing, and contacting emergency services to a praying app that supports various religions. They've had over seventy thousand downloads and have plans for major expansion.

Juliette Brindack: She started the social-networking site Miss O and Friends to help tweens build their self-esteem when she was only sixteen years old. It all started with some sketches she did when she was ten of what she thought "cool girls" looked like. Millions of adolescents visit her site every month to participate in message boards, quizzes, games, and music. She published a book called *Miss O & Friends: Write On! The Miss O & Friends Collection of Rockin' Fiction* and has plans for many more in the future.

10

Visionaries

Do you have an idea you are extremely passionate about? Do you dream about the future and imagine what changes will take place as you get older? Visionaries aren't happy just going with the flow; they want to create something new. Walt Disney is a great example of a visionary. He had a clear vision when he set out to create a magical place for people of all ages to enjoy animation. Do you think some people thought his idea was overly ambitious or crazy? Of course they did, but he was fully committed to his dream. Visionaries lead us with their advances in entertainment, technology, healthcare, and science. Their great imagination, determination, and passion create some pretty amazing things!

TEDxTeen

Do you want to know where all of the future leaders your age hang out? Try TEDxTeen! This once-a-year event brings together the world's newest changemakers and thinkers. They are leaders specializing in every subject, from science to the arts. You can attend the events in person or follow the conference at tedxteen.com, where you can watch talks, join in on discussions, and get more information about the speakers. TEDxTeen gives leaders in all industries a chance to share ideas and become inspired.

SPOTLIGHT

Steve Jobs

When we think of visionaries, it's hard not to think of Steve Jobs and Apple Computers. Born in 1955 in San Francisco, California, and raised by his adoptive parents in Silicon Valley, Jobs was exposed early to technology. He spent his evenings attending lectures by Hewlett-Packard scientists and wasn't shy about asking questions. In 1974, he dropped out of Reed College and reconnected with his high school friend Stephen Wozniak. Together in Jobs's family garage they developed the Apple I computer. He was determined to bring personal computers to the masses.

He cofounded Apple Computers in the 1970s, was kicked out of the company by his own board of directors in the 1980s, and returned as the company CEO in 1997. He didn't let his time away from Apple

Computers go to waste. He started the companies Pixar and NeXT. Pixar brought computer animation to the big screen and is responsible for some of the most famous animated movies of all time: *Toy Story*, *Cars*, and *Monsters, Inc.* NeXT built powerful computers and developed operating systems. Apple bought NeXT and welcomed Jobs back to the company.

Steve Jobs's leadership style was governed by ambition, a clear vision, and enthusiasm. No matter what obstacles were put in his way he continued to work hard and pursue his goals. His ambition brought the technology products like the iMac, iBook, iPod, iPhone, and iPad. A clear vision created one of the most successful marketing campaigns of all time. Every product, store, website design, and advertisement is streamlined and sends a clear message. His enthusiasm was contagious—every new product launch or update causes people to line up outside Apple Store doors to be the first to own the new thing. It's become a status symbol to be the first to have the newest iPhone. Jobs made technology cool!

  Quiz

Are You a Visionary?

Most visionaries share some personality traits. Read through the following list and write the statements that apply to you on a separate piece of paper.

★ You like to think outside of the box for solutions to problems.

★ You don't get caught up in the details but prefer to look at the big picture.

- ★ You notice when things are soon to become outdated and wonder what's coming next.

- ★ You look toward the future and don't linger in the past.

- ★ You like to challenge people's ideas.

- ★ You see things differently from most people, and sometimes your ideas seem a little "out there" to people.

- ★ You've got a ton of great ideas for inventions.

- ★ You have a wonderful imagination.

- ★ You have business leaders, inventors, or scientists you look up to.

- ★ You think anything is possible.

The visionary starts with a clean sheet of paper, and reimagines the world.[1]
—MALCOLM GLADWELL, BESTSELLING AUTHOR, JOURNALIST, AND SPEAKER

★✪★✪★✪★✪★✪★✪★✪★✪★

Name: Chris Bergman
Job: Founder and CEO of ChoreMonster

Chris Bergman and Paul Armstrong set out in 2011 to make doing chores a positive experience. Most people wouldn't use the words *fun* and *chores* in the same sentence, but they probably haven't tried using the ChoreMonster app. The app lets parents set chore lists, assign rewards and points for completion, and check their children's progress. It also has fun monster animation and awards for kids and lets them manage their lists of chores. Who wouldn't want to earn cool stuff or work toward fun activities?

Describe ChoreMonster.
ChoreMonster is a suite of web and mobile apps that allow parents and kids to actually enjoy doing chores. Kids gain points and turn them in for real-life rewards like an hour of Minecraft, a new toy, or even a canoe trip. Kids also get to collect interactive monsters! For every chore that a child completes, that kid gets a ticket to the monster carnival, where they can earn over one hundred different interactive monsters or a consolation prize such as a jar of farts.

How did ChoreMonster get started?
ChoreMonster began when my wife was pregnant with our first child. I was thinking a lot about how to make sure that our son grows up in a positive, joyful home. I am someone who loves his work and wanted him to know how work can be rewarding and fun. Meanwhile, my business partner, Paul, was drawing monsters with his twelve-year-old son. We took the two ideas, combined them, and came up with an amazing app.

What are some of the challenges of starting a new business?
Starting a new business is an incredibly difficult task. It takes a lot of effort to get a tech company off the ground. One of the early challenges is capital. We had to find investors who believed in our idea and mission. Once enough capital was raised, we had to find talent. Searching for the most creative people in the world can be a daunting task, but thankfully due to social media and previous relationships, we were able to build a team that could execute our vision.

How do you keep your team motivated?

We're a company dedicated to making work fun, and we take that to heart. Around long coding stints and piles of email, you'll regularly find our team playing foosball or board games. I think it's important to have a team that works well together and knows how to communicate. By being efficient in our communication, we make sure the work we're doing never becomes stale.

What are the most important leadership skills to have when operating a start-up?

The absolutely most important skill to have is honesty. A leader's yes must mean yes and no must mean no. Without character, you lose trust; without trust, you lose any chance at leadership.

What advice would you give teens who would like to start a business?

Go do it. Right now. Go start building things and creating. Don't wait until you have all the skills "needed" to do it. You can learn along the way. Actually, that's typically the best way to learn.

What leaders do you admire?

I'd have to say that Walt and Roy Disney are the two leaders that I admire the most. Prior to Bill Gates, Steve Jobs, or Larry Ellison, the Disney brothers created technology needed to execute their vision of multipanel animated stories with synced audio. These guys knew how to innovate well before computers!

✪✪✪✪✪✪✪✪✪✪✪✪✪✪✪✪✪✪✪✪✪✪✪✪✪

Do You Have What It Takes to Be a Visionary?

Are you willing to take risks?

Do you trust your judgment?

Can you translate your idea into a real object or goal?

Are you willing to stick it out even when things get tough?

Can you turn failure into something positive by learning from your mistakes?

Can you ask for help when you need it?

Are you okay with people doubting your idea?

If you answered yes to those questions, then you are ready to put together a plan to make your vision become a reality. Being a visionary is a lot of work because you are doing something no one has done before. You are the pioneer in your field, so you'll have to start from scratch on your idea. This is exciting too because you are doing something new. Who knows? Your idea could change history!

★★★★★★★★★★★★★★★★

Name: Kajmere Houchins
Age: 14
Job (when not studying!): Founder of the Power Cave

Fourteen-year-old Kajmere Houchins wasn't supposed to live to see her teen years. Diagnosed with cancer for the first time at age six, she's beaten the disease three times. At the age of nine, with a grim diagnosis, she decided to make a bucket list of things she wanted to do and set out to do them. She was determined to give her life meaning. Bullied at school, she decided to take action by creating an antibullying petition. She presented her petition to the Washington Board of Education and it was adopted as law. Her website, the Power Cave, empowers teens to fight for what they believe in. As a teen role model and leader, she's spoken at the TEDxTeen 2014 conference, given antibullying speeches at high schools, and was honored at We Day 2014 in front of nearly seventeen thousand people.

What have you learned by starting the Power Cave?
The most important thing I have learned is I can help people. I have also learned about responsibility and how much work goes into doing something great. I have met some really awesome young people and adults. I am always surprised when I find out they know who I am. I have had people send me their personal stories, so I've learned about what other kids are going through and how I have been able to help them in times of need. I have learned I can do this. At some point, I thought it was going to be too hard, too much work, but I know I can do this.

Where do you think all of your self-confidence comes from?
It's funny, because most people think I am a really confident, super social person, and the truth is I am naturally a little shy and quiet and like to be alone. Confidence is something I work at. I have to try really hard to be the person who can step on a stage. I'm actually very scared. I take deep breaths, smile, and say a prayer. That's why I tell people they have to make a conscious choice to be a better person, to do good things, and to make hard decisions, because I do every time I have to go and talk to people.

How do you think having a passion for social injustice has affected how you view yourself?
I always knew I was passionate about people and was frustrated with how my friends acted and people around me acted in certain social situations. It wasn't until I went to a weeklong

camp called the Youth Organizing Institute through the Seattle Young People's Project (of which I am a board member) that I had the vocabulary and the format to see that I was frustrated with social justice issues. I have friends who are homeless, so this issue affects me profoundly. My parents struggle to give me things, so poverty is an issue that I am passionate about. I am multiracial, and my friends come from diverse backgrounds, so racial injustice is also important to me. I guess more than anything, I have found I am one of millions of people who are affected by social injustice. I don't think I knew that before. It may be because my parents just wanted me to be happy and not worry about things. I think if I have knowledge early, I can begin affecting change early; I can inspire friends and do something. I view myself not as a victim but as a changemaker.

How has having a passion helped you to make friends?
First, I tried to be part of the "in" crowd and realized the "in" crowd wasn't for me. Not at my school anyway. Because of my cancer treatment, I spent more time around adults than kids, so I grew up faster. I've had to deal with issues most people my age haven't, so I have a different perspective than most young people. I have lost friends, and I have made friends. Over the last year, and since I started really pushing for change regarding antibullying, I have found that I connect with other shy, bullied students who just want to do something to change their surroundings and feel supported. I have lots of people who reach out to me online, ask me for advice, and have flocked to me at school. The best thing is I have created boundaries for myself, with friends, and at school. I am not just liked, I am respected. And there is a huge difference. I don't care if people like me, but I do hope they respect me. I am proud to be different. I am okay being part of my own crowd. I know the friends I make already know who I am and what I stand for and against. They are often more genuine, because they know who I am.

What's the most exciting moment you've experienced since you started the Power Cave?

Being invited to speak in New York City with TEDxTeen 2014. I have done some awesome things, but this by far was the most exciting. I feel blessed and honored to have been invited to be part of something so big and with such great people. From beginning to end, the process was exciting and opened so many doors for me. The event was filled with other amazing young people doing awesome things in their own communities and some in the world. They paid for our flight and accommodations, and even though I had flown before I had never been anywhere like New York City. I don't know if there is any place like New York City. I met Nile Rogers, Q-tip, GZA, and people from other great organizations. It was awesome to be around people my age that are so passionate about doing good. Being streamed on MTV online was cool too.

I also participated in We Day Seattle 2014. I was called onstage and honored in front of seventeen thousand young leaders in my state. They all know who I am now. It was mind-blowing to be in a place with that many pumped-up teens and young people all listening to my story! Seeing myself on *Seventeen.com*—that was so cool! And on the front pages of newspapers! *Wow!*

What are your goals for the Power Cave?

Well, I want to work with my mom and other people to make sure the Power Cave is sustainable. So we don't all just get bored and say, "Okay, we're done." I see this turning into a larger organization over time and reaching people on an international scale. People all over the world. I want to see the Power Cave in physical form pulling in young people from all over and putting them to work to make change. I would eventually like to have a space for people to meet and collaborate with other like-minded organizations on large community projects. Also, we would like to organize a teen summit where young people can come listen, participate, and learn from each other.

Challenge
Create Your Own Vision

Sometimes it's difficult to get the creative juices flowing. Here's a little exercise to get you started. Each challenge includes an example of someone else's vision for the same category. Have fun with this. Not every idea has to be super serious. You can come up with anything from flying saucers to rechewable gum. It's your vision and your ideas!

Challenge #1: What is an invention that would make homework easier for you and your friends? Example: In 1997, a math teacher wanted to make learning math more fun for kids, so she started the website coolmath .com. Since then, millions of people from age three to one hundred have learned new math concepts through online lessons, activities, and games.

Challenge #2: During the school year you have to get up and get ready pretty early in the morning. What is something that would make your morning routine faster? Example: Do you see a robot getting you dressed while you sleep, an automatic breakfast maker, or a new way to take a shower?

Challenge #3: Some forward-thinking companies have come up with ways to integrate philanthropy into their business models. Think of a way you could do this while operating a lemonade stand. Example: Ben & Jerry's ice cream company has always been a leader when it comes to figuring out a way to use the company to help other people. The flavor Chocolate Fudge Brownie contained brownies made by homeless and unemployed people in New York.

Challenge #4: Software applications, apps, are small programs for cell phones or tablets that perform specific functions. Come up with an idea for an app you could use in your everyday life. Example: Shazam allows a person to push a button on a cell phone screen to get the name and artist of the song playing on the radio.

Warning: imaginary visions will not work unless you act on them.

★★★★★★★★★★★★★★★★★★

Name: Megan Grassell
Age: 19
Job (when not studying!): Founder of Yellowberry

At age seventeen, Megan Grassell was not happy with the lingerie selection available to preteen girls, so instead of complaining about the problem, she decided to solve it. Her goal was to create cute and age-appropriate bras. Using the fundraising website Kickstarter she raised $42,000 in thirty days from over one thousand donors to start her business. Now, two years later, her business is thriving. Each bra comes in a bright color and includes an empowering message. Read on to learn how Megan started a company while completing her senior year in high school.

Describe Yellowberry.
Yellowberry is much more than just a bra company; it is a brand that stands to empower girls with self-confidence and positive self-esteem so they know that they can do anything they set their minds to.

How did it get started?

Yellowberry started after I went shopping with my younger sister, Mary Margaret, to buy her very first bras at the age of thirteen. We couldn't find anything that wasn't padded, push-up, super sexualized bras or the very boring sports bras at the opposite end of the spectrum. All we wanted was a cute, comfortable bra for her to wear that fit her body. At the time, there were none, so I decided that if no one else would fix this problem, then I would make this bra.

How did you manage high school and starting a company at the same time?

I didn't, really. I had a very difficult time balancing the demanding schoolwork with my entrepreneurial goals. Part of that was because of the timing: applying to school the first semester of my senior year, studying for exams, etc. But the second semester, when things were really, really busy, I spent every waking minute working on Yellowberry and, in turn, not working on my schoolwork. It was one of the first times when I realized I had to choose either maintaining my good grades or letting them slip to email customers, pack boxes, and build the Yellowberry community. I chose to run the company and was catapulted into a job that I am absolutely obsessed with!

What are your strengths as a leader?

I am a very passionate person, and I think that that is clear to those around me. With that passion, I have a clear vision for the direction in which Yellowberry is going. The people I do work and interact with see that in me, and I hope it sparks something in them too: a large ambition, a very strong work ethic, and a great sense of pride in what we do.

What are your biggest challenges as a leader?

I expect a lot from myself as an individual. I have to realize that sometimes the expectations I have for myself may be different from what someone else expects of themselves. So, I think that being a leader is not being able to tell someone what to do but leading by exemplifying exactly what needs to happen.

What leaders do you look up to?

This question brings two people immediately to mind: Mindy Kaling and Scott Hirschfield. Mindy Kaling is absolutely one of the people I look up to in basically every single way. She is hysterical, talented, and able to be a strong woman in charge of an amazing career and group of people (*The Office* is also my favorite television show ever!). Scott Hirschfield was the headmaster of my high school in Jackson, Wyoming. He founded the school Jackson Hole Community School for grades nine through twelve. He is without a doubt one of the kindest and most selfless people I have ever come across. His staff of teachers were people passionate about teaching calculus, Russian history, or English literature. The school in its entirety absolutely loved Scott (he left the school after ten years; my graduating class was his final year), and we were all inspired by him as a person to be a part of the school.

What advice would you give teens who are interested in starting companies?

One, I think that it's really important to understand that there are always people who have much more knowledge and experience, and you will meet them as you move forward—and that's a great thing! Find those people, reach out to them, take them out to coffee, and seek advice and mentorship from them. I have come to realize that is [one] of the most important elements of business. Two, always ask questions! Three, as a young person starting a company, you have to work very hard to earn your own credibility. But once you do, it's one of the most rewarding positions to be in, to have proved yourself right!

❂❂❂❂❂❂❂❂❂❂❂❂❂❂❂❂❂❂❂❂❂❂❂❂

11

Get Industrious

So, now that you've decided you want to be a leader, what do you do? It may seem overwhelming to start planning your career while you're busy with school, friends, and activities. Don't get nervous; get excited! You can prepare for your future while going about your daily routine. Every day you make decisions. You choose what to wear, when to do your homework, and how to spend your allowance. Branch out from there and develop your public speaking skills by participating in class, take the lead on a project, and work out a budget for your spending money. Leadership opportunities are everywhere. Enjoy learning new ways to take charge!

If you want to be a leader, be prepared to work your way to the top. Some people may feel that aiming for a leadership role is too ambitious. These are some objections you may hear:

It takes many, many years to work your way to the top.

What are the chances you will become the next Oprah Winfrey or president of the United States?

You need to be rich to become a leader.

You're not outgoing enough to be a leader.

If you are going to be a leader, you need an advanced degree.

One way to have the discussion about your leadership interests is to do your homework. Read about all the many ways you can become a leader. People will take you more seriously if you've done your research. Have a game plan on how you're going to develop the skills you need to succeed in your career interest.

How Can You Learn More about Leadership Opportunities?

Find a mentor. Anytime you are around leaders, ask them questions, see if you can watch them work, and seek their advice.

Look into clubs at your schools and compare student-run activities with ones run by faculty. How do the leadership styles differ?

Learn from the best by reading books about famous leaders in history.

Read the business section of your newspaper for profiles of local and national leaders.

Check for a speaker series at the nearby college. Colleges often invite guest speakers in various career fields to speak. Most of these are open to the public and free of charge.

Good vs. Bad Leaders

We've all read stories, seen movies, and learned through history the effect bad leaders can have on those around them. Some people let power go to their heads and would rather demand respect than earn it. A great leader is not driven by ego but is more concerned about the welfare of the team. When you inspire your team members, they will want to work harder for you and the organization. This benefits everybody. Read the following lists to see what makes a good leader versus a bad leader. Don't let yourself fall into the trap of being the bossy boss!

Good Leaders

Provide tools and training to help people do their jobs and increase their knowledge base

Recognize people's achievements and let them know

Treat their teams like they want their customers treated

Are great listeners

Let people do their jobs without interfering

Enjoy getting input from their team

Bad Leaders

Control people and don't trust them to do their jobs

Blame the team when things go wrong

Are unavailable or "too busy" for their teams

Boss people around

Think they are better than everyone else

Believe they are smarter than their team members, so they never accept input

It's All about the First Impression

If you want to go out there and dominate your field, then you need to know how to make a great first impression. If you make a strong first impression, then you will immediately gain people's trust and respect. A bad impression takes a long time to overcome, and as a leader, you want to inspire people and their loyalty. Here are some key tips on how you can get off on the right foot as a leader:

Be sincere when you meet someone. Nobody likes someone who acts fake, looks bored, or can't make eye contact.

Be friendly to the people you lead. This may sound like common sense, but many times leaders are so focused on work that they forget to engage with people. A short conversation or a quick lunch can go a long way.

Be a listener. Don't talk over your team. Take the time to hear and understand what they are saying. The best ideas come from listening.

Give credit where credit is due. Using people's talents and rewarding them are signs of a strong leader.

Have a sense of humor. Things don't always go as planned, so being able to laugh is really important.

Admit your mistakes. People will respect you if you are honest about your faults.

Lead by example. You set the tone for your organization, so bring a great attitude and work ethic to every meeting.

Know how to keep people motivated. Give people compliments and rewards. Everyone likes to feel encouraged and appreciated.

Movies on Leadership

Movies are a fun way to see leaders in action and a great way to see the many different ways people lead. These movies represent leaders from the 1950s to the modern day. Do you see a difference in how leaders are portrayed over the years? What other differences can you spot? You may notice that the leaders of today are shown as being of a variety of backgrounds. Watch a movie and then write down what you've learned. Even bad leaders have a lot to teach us, so grab some popcorn and enjoy the show!

★ *Amazing Grace*, 2006

★ *Apollo 13*, 1995

★ *Chariots of Fire*, 1981

★ *Dead Poets Society*, 1989

★ *Finding Forrester*, 2000

★ *Freedom Writers*, 2007

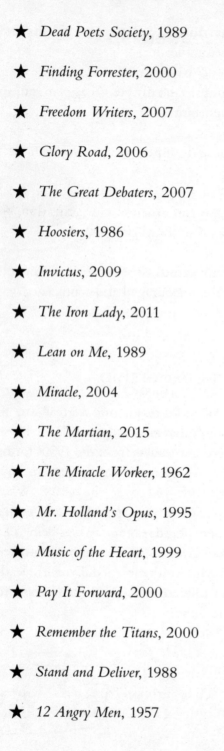

★ *Glory Road*, 2006

★ *The Great Debaters*, 2007

★ *Hoosiers*, 1986

★ *Invictus*, 2009

★ *The Iron Lady*, 2011

★ *Lean on Me*, 1989

★ *Miracle*, 2004

★ *The Martian*, 2015

★ *The Miracle Worker*, 1962

★ *Mr. Holland's Opus*, 1995

★ *Music of the Heart*, 1999

★ *Pay It Forward*, 2000

★ *Remember the Titans*, 2000

★ *Stand and Deliver*, 1988

★ *12 Angry Men*, 1957

Books on Leadership

7 Habits of Highly Effective Teens **by Sean Covey (2014):** This book is aimed at teaching you to set goals, plan for your future, and make the tough decisions to be successful.

The Alchemist **by Paulo Coelho (1988):** This inspirational novel about a shepherd boy has been translated into seventy-one languages. The boy's journey shows the power of dreams and trusting your heart.

Drive: The Surprising Truth about What Motivates Us **by Daniel H. Pink (2011):** This book focuses on the principles that motivate people to be in charge of their own lives, to create new things, and to have a life purpose. Find out what motivates you!

How to Win Friends and Influence People **by Dale Carnegie (1998):** This is a great book to read for anyone who wants to improve communication skills. A great leader needs to be able to give direction, feedback, and praise. Carnegie's book gives lots of tips on how to build a positive team with open communication.

Questions of Character: Illuminating the Heart of Leadership through Literature **by Joseph L. Badaracco Jr. (2006):** The author uses fictional characters to teach lessons about good leadership skills and leadership mistakes. He demonstrates this through eight challenges that test people's characters and how they respond to those challenges.

The Teen Business Manual: A Guide for Teen Leadership and Entrepreneurship, **by James Scott (2014):** Do you have a great idea for starting a business or a school group? This book gives you all the tools you need to do everything from write a business plan to give a presentation.

***Teen Leadership Revolution: How Ordinary Teens Become Extraordinary Leaders* by Tom Thelen (2012):** Why do some high school students graduate and go on to become successful adults while others peak in high school? This book explores four different character levels of strong leadership: rights, relationships, results, and respect.

***Tribes: We Need You to Lead Us* by Seth Godin (2008):** This book uses case studies to demonstrate the power of tribes. People with a common interest and a strong leader can make positive changes.

***True North: Discover Your Authentic Leadership* by Bill George and Peter Sims (2007):** Based on interviews with 125 leaders, this book focuses on knowing who you are, defining your leadership values and motivation, and building a team.

***The Truth about Leadership: The No-Fads, Heart-of-the-Matter Facts You Need to Know* by James M. Kouzes and Barry Z. Posner (2010):** This book was written with the new leader in mind. By the end of the book, you will know the ten essential lessons you need to master to be an effective leader.

***What It Takes to Be #1* by Vince Lombardi (2012):** Vince Lombardi was one of the most motivational football coaches in history. This book examines his top values of commitment, discipline, excellence, mental toughness, habit, faith, passion, results, and truth.

***Who Moved My Cheese?* by Spencer Johnson (1998):** Are you good at adapting to change, or would you prefer it if everything stayed the same? Leaders need to know when to make changes and how to navigate their teams through them. This funny book is a great resource for people facing new and unexpected situations.

Other Leadership Resources

CIA: cia.gov

Environmental Protection Agency: epa.gov/myenvironment

Everyday Ambassador: everydayambassador.org

FBI: fbiagentedu.org; fbinaa.org

National Leadership Conference: nslcleaders.org

ROTC: rotc.com

US Military Service: military.com

12

Glossary

accountable. Taking responsibility, or being held responsible.

advanced degree. A college degree beyond an undergraduate degree.

advocates. An active group that provides or seeks support.

appeal. To have a case or decision looked at again by someone with higher authority.

bill. A proposal to the government to change or make a law.

budget. Money set aside for a purpose.

cash flow. Money that moves into and out of a business.

collaborate. To work as a group of people.

communication skills. Ability to express yourself.

connector. Someone who brings people together for a useful purpose.

conservation. Preserving something from loss, destruction, or depletion.

delegate. To put someone in charge of a project, task, or assignment.

democracy. A system that's ruled by all people and is based on equality.

empower. To give power or permission to someone.

entry-level. A beginner-level job where someone can gain experience before moving on to a higher position.

feedback. A response to an activity.

founder. The person who starts a new business.

fundraising. Raising money for a particular cause.

goal. What you want to achieve.

grassroots. The beginning of something, which usually starts out very basic or simple.

grit. Spirit and determination.

guru. A spiritual leader.

hierarchy. Things arranged in order by rank.

humanitarian. Person who improves the lives and welfare of people.

humanity. The quality of life for all humans.

idealism. Belief in a higher purpose or goal.

impact. To affect something or someone.

infrastructure. The basis or framework for a system.

innovator. Introduces something brand new.

intolerant. Not respectful of another person's belief or value.

lobby group. Individuals or special interest groups who attempt to influence government decisions and laws.

mentor. A sponsor, supporter, or teacher.

mission. A goal or purpose.

multicultural. Representing different cultures.

networking. Assisting other people and asking for help.

nonprofit. A business not started for the money but for the public interest.

opportunity. A chance to achieve a goal or have success.

outreach. Services provided.

performance. How someone completes an activity or job.

philanthropy. The act of helping other people or social causes.

preserve. To keep safe or take care of.

productivity. How fast or well something is done or created.

resources. Money, people, or things that help someone do a job.

social activism. Taking an active part in preserving or helping a cause.

solution. Answer to a problem.

sustainable. Using resources so they will last a long time.

tenacity. Not giving up when things get tough.

unified. Brought together as one.

vision. The ability to think up future ideas or inventions.

NOTES

Chapter 1

1. Jack Welch, quoted in Kevin Kruse, "100 Best Quotes on Leadership," *Forbes*, October 16, 2012, http://www.forbes.com/sites/kevinkruse/2012/10/16/quotes-on-leadership.

Chapter 2

1. Rosalynn Carter, quoted in Kevin Kruse, "100 Best Quotes on Leadership," *Forbes*, October 16, 2012, http://www.forbes.com/sites/KevinKruse/2012/10/16/quotes-on-leadership.

2. "United States Government: Judicial Branch—The Supreme Court," Ducksters, last modified July 20, 2015, http://www.ducksters.com/history/us_judicial_branch.php.

3. Emma Watson, "Gender Equality Is Your Issue Too," speech by UN Women Goodwill Ambassador at special event for the HeForShe campaign, United Nations Headquarters, NY, September 20, 2014, transcript, http://www.unwomen.org/en/news/stories/2014/9/emma-watson-gender-equality-is-your-issue-too.

Chapter 3

1. Brad Thor, quoted in "Law Enforcement Quotes," BrainyQuote.com, accessed October 14, 2014, http://www.brainyquote.com/quotes/keywords/law_enforcement.html.

Chapter 4

1. Rosalyn Carter, quoted in Madhura Pandit, "Leadership Quotes by Women," Buzzle, last modified December 6, 2012, http://www.buzzle.com/articles/leadership-quotes-by-women.html.

2. Bill Gates, quoted in Ben Lillie, "Married and Working Together to Solve Inequality: Bill and Melinda Gates at TED2014," *TEDBlog*, March 18, 2014, http://blog.ted.com/married-and-working-together-to-solve-inequality-bill-and-melinda-gates-at-ted2014/.

3. St. Jude Children's Research Hospital, "Fifty Fabulous Years," *Promise*, Spring 2012, https://www.stjude.org/about-st-jude/stories/promise-magazine/spring-2012/fifty-fabulous-years.html.

Chapter 5

1. Dianne Feinstein, quoted in "Dianne Feinstein Quotes," BrainyQuote.com, accessed November 7, 2014, http://www.brainyquote.com/quotes/quotes/d/diannefein163960.html.

2. "Peace Corps Today," Peace Corps, last modified October 8, 2014, http://www.peacecorps.gov/today/.

Chapter 6

1. Russell Simmons, quoted in "Russell Simmons Quotes," BrainyQuote.com, accessed September 8, 2014, http://www.brainyquote.com/quotes/authors/r/russell_simmons.html.

2. National Football League, "'Bill Parcells: Reflections on a Life in Football' Airs on NFLN," NFL.com, November 8, 2010, http://www.nfl.com/nflnetwork/story/09000d5d81bf75c9/article/bill-parcells-reflections-on-a-life-in-football-airs-on-nfln.

Chapter 7

1. Martin Luther King, Jr., quoted in "Martin Luther King, Jr. Quotes," BrainyQuote.com, accessed September 22, 2014, http://www.brainyquote.com/quotes/authors/m/martin_luther_king_jr.html.

Chapter 8

1. Margaret Mead, quoted in "Environmental Quotes," BrainyQuote.com, accessed October 14, 2014, http://www.brainyquote.com/quotes/topics/topic_environmental.html.

Chapter 9

1. Andrew Carnegie, quoted in "Best Leadership Quotes," *Leaders Digest*, October 11, 2014, http://leadersdigest.me/2014/10/11/best -leadership-quotes.

Chapter 10

1. Malcolm Gladwell, quoted in "Visionary Quotes," BrainyQuote.com, accessed October 14, 2014, http://www.brainyquote.com/quotes /keywords/visionary.html.

Chapter 11

1. Theodore Roosevelt, quoted in Kevin Kruse, "100 Best Quotes on Leadership," *Forbes*, October 16, 2012, http://www.forbes.com/sites /kevinkruse/2012/10/16/quotes-on-leadership.